Before the days of hybrid corn, your great-great-grandpa Knud Oster hand-picked the biggest and best ears from the harvest. From those ears he selected kernels for the following year's seed.

Those ears containing the best kernels were carefully hung by their husks to dry for the winter.

In the early spring the best looking kernels were shelled from the ears. They became the hope for the new year. You are one of God's men who offer hope for the next generation.

This book contains seeds of truth, some of them passed from Knud Oster to James Oster to Harland Oster to Merrill Oster and now on to you.

Truth stored in one's mind, however, only puffs a person's image of himself. Truth put to use with discretion in life becomes wisdom in action... offering hope and direction to others.

From *Father to Son: Becoming a Man of Honor*

The Companion Volume to
Mother to Daughter: Becoming a Woman of Honor

BECOMING

A MAN OF HONOR

Merrill J.
Oster

Published by
HERE'S LIFE PUBLISHERS, INC.
P.O. Box 1576
San Bernardino, CA 92402

HLP Product No. 951947

Library of Congress Cataloging-in-Publication Data

   Oster, Merrill J., 1940-
    Father to son : becoming a man of honor / Merrill J. Oster.
     p. cm.
    Summary: A father advises his son, a young man coming of age, on
spiritual and social issues in such areas as relationships, goals, inner
life, and preparedness.
    ISBN 0-89840-192-5 (pbk.)
    1. Young men — Religious life. 2. Young men — Conduct of life.
[1. Christain life. 2. Conduct of life.]   I. Title.
BV4541.2.O88   1988   87-18790
248.8'32 — dc 19   CIP
                                                 AC

Unless designated otherwise, Scripture quotations are from *The Living
Bible,* © 1971 by Tyndale House Publishers, Wheaton, Illinois.

Scripture quotations designated NASB are from *The New Amercan Standard Bible,* © The Lockman Foundation 1960, 1962, 1963, 1968, 1971, 1972,
1975, 1977.

Scripture quotations designated KJV are from the King James Version of
the Bible.

For More Information, Write:

L.I.F.E.—P.O. Box A399, Sydney South 2000, Australia
Campus Crusade for Christ of Canada—Box 300, Vancouver, B.C., V6C 2X3, Canada
Campus Crusade for Christ—Pearl Assurance House, 4 Temple Row, Birmingham, B2 5HG, England
Lay Institute for Evangelism—P.O. Box 8786, Auckland 3, New Zealand
Campus Crusade for Christ—P.O. Box 240, Colombo Court Post Office, Singapore 9117
Great Commission Movement of Nigeria—P.O. Box 500, Jos, Plateau State Nigeria, West Africa
Campus Crusade for Christ International—Arrowhead Springs, San Bernardino, CA 92414, U.S.A.

To Carol, my wife, whom God has used to shape our family through her admonition, love, patience and faithful service.

How blessed is the man who does not
walk in the counsel of the wicked,
Nor stand in the path of sinners,
Nor sit in the seat of scoffers!
But his delight is in the law of the LORD,
And in His law he meditates day and night.
And he will be like a tree firmly planted
by streams of water,
Which yields its fruit in its season,
And its leaf does not wither;
And in whatever he does, he prospers.

Psalm 1:1—3

Contents

A MAN OF HONOR

How Seeds of Truth Take Root

They are like trees along a river bank bearing luscious fruit each season without fail. Their leaves shall never wither, and all they do shall prosper.
(Psalm 1:3)

Before the days of hybrid corn, your great-great-grandpa Knud Oster hand-picked the biggest and best ears from the harvest. From those ears he selected kernels for the following year's seed.

Those ears containing the best kernels were carefully hung by their husks to dry for the winter.

In the early spring the best looking kernels were shelled from the ears. They became the hope for the new year. You, David, are one of God's men who offer hope for the next generation.

This book contains seeds of truth, some of them passed from Knud Oster to James Oster to Harland Oster to Merrill Oster and now on to you.

Truth stored in one's mind, however, only puffs a person's image of himself. Truth put to use with discretion in life becomes wisdom in action, offering hope and direction to others.

Obviously, this book is no substitute for the ultimate source of truth. God has guided the generations before you, and is available to you if you daily seek His counsel.

There are seeds of truth already alive in your life. Cultivate them through practice. You will crowd out all the weeds of despair, confusion and chaos which characterize the lives of so many around you in today's world.

Last night the April temperature dropped to an all-time low of twenty-five degrees. But today the sun came out and caused the new buds on the oak just outside the kitchen window to push the last of last year's leaves off the tree.

A new season is upon us.

The new bud symbolizes your entry into the world.

This is the spring of your life. Lying ahead of you are the winds of change, the storms of challenge, the victorious sunny days and a few gloomy days as well.

As a man seeking to learn from God's Word and to follow His paths, you will be like the tree planted near the river in Psalm 1. Fed by a deep root system which has been developing since you were born, you will grow as long as you tap the principles of the Bible, the "river of living waters."

The pages in this book tell you about some of the seeds already rooted and growing in your life. Those roots have established you and will now sustain you.

You have been a marked man from your early days. Handsome. Talented. Well-liked. Intelligent. Inquisitive. Interested in others. God-led.

The world is crying out for men with these attributes. Much will be required of you.

To date, your mom and I have had a big influence in seeing that the growth of your roots was not impeded. We've fertilized and watered.

Where you go from here will be determined largely by how much you allow God to use the bundle of resources packaged as David M. Oster.

You're on your own, son. God is your partner. The Lord is your shepherd. The Holy Spirit is your guide.

Mom and I hereby retire to the role of friend, consultant, coach and prayer partner.

1
PERSPECTIVE
❧

The Secret of a Positive, Fulfilling Approach

But all these things that I once thought very worthwhile — now I've thrown them all away so that I can put my trust and hope in Christ alone.
(Philippians 3:7)

Chen Zing Geng is a Chinese farmer I met a few years ago on a study trip to China. After showing our group around the commune, he motioned me aside. I followed him to the patio of his house. Through the interpreter, and with body language that communicates faster than the spoken word, he told me the exciting story of his life. With a big sweep of his arm he indicated that all that land out there belonged to "the people." Then with a little twitch of the finger he indicated that a small one-sixth of an acre plot was his.

I asked him what he was going to do with the income from the plot. With great excitement in his eyes, he told me that at the end of the season he would have accumulated enough money for his very own bicycle.

Whenever I am tempted to feel down about the agricultural reversals which wiped out most of our land equity, I remember Chen Zing Geng. That helps me keep things in perspective.

Perspective. That's the point. Are we able to see the big picture to keep things in the proper perspective?

One day in my concern for Great-Grandpa Oster's welfare, I probed into his financial affairs to see if he needed any help. "Help? Me? Nah! Ma and me never had it better. Every month we get the yellow check, and then we get a green check. They add up to $240 a month. What's a man my age need with more money than that?"

By my standards, Grandpa was economically deprived. He drove his hand-painted $125 car, raised a garden and a few chickens and lived well within his means. From his perspective, he was well off.

Few people get and keep things in perspective, the right relationship to each other. As humans we tend to focus on one or two issues at a time and make them the big deals of our life. One of your challenges will be to keep the competing elements in life in perspective . . . in your perspective and in God's perspective.

Perspective demands reference points. As Christians, we see a different time line. The horizon for us doesn't end with life on this earth; it just goes on, and on, and on.

Because our perspective is different, our decisions will be different. We will place different values on certain things in life. We quickly dismiss certain ideas, thoughts and distractions which occupy large amounts of some people's time.

The ultimate loss of perspective is a life lived in despair, one dominated by feelings of insignificance or hopelessness. From God's perspective, we are of infinite value, with an important role to play in life, and with eternal goals in mind. The world needs to see this story lived out by men and women who have their "heads screwed on right."

Keep Your Attitude Positive

A positive attitude helps you maintain a proper perspective in life and acts as a filtering mechanism for your mind. If you filter incoming facts from a positive frame of reference, the way you view the world will be different from the way those people who are without hope and without Christ (and who are, therefore, negative) view the world.

For those moments when thoughts of discouragement do flood in, and you think of abandoning your plans, Paul has this word:

> And now, brothers, as I close this letter let me say this one more thing: Fix your thoughts on what is true and good and right. Think about things that are pure and lovely, and dwell on the fine, good things in others. Think about all you can praise God for and be glad about. Keep putting into practice all you learned from me and saw me doing, and the God of peace will be with you (Philippians 4:8,9).

A positive attitude formed on the base of Christ's strength will not let you down. However, popular motivational speakers who lecture from a base built on humanism or the "human potential movement" will, in the end, leave you unfulfilled. Empty. The typical "positive attitude" sales meeting speech is built on how we can work our way out of circumstances by applying our brain. Many people find temporary encouragement even in this type of environment.

How much stronger the encouragement which comes from a positive attitude based on Christ's power. Then the credit for any subsequent success goes to Him, rather than inflating your own ego.

A positive attitude takes even the negative facts and finds a positive way to look at them. Some incorrectly say a positive attitude is really "looking at the world through rose-colored glasses."

But to the Christian, a positive attitude is based on the assurance that "all things work together for good." We can rejoice in negative circumstances, knowing that God is using them to develop us.

In the midst of the recent agricultural crisis, I met a farmer who had lost everything. He commented, with peace in his heart, "You know, it has been tough, but through it all our family has come closer to each other. And closer to God."

His positive attitude helped pull the family together. Even though he was now driving a truck instead of being in his preferred farming career, his attitude was, "We'll be OK. Our family is in good health, and we have never missed a meal."

His view was not one of unrealistically viewing his situation through "rose-colored glasses," but of acknowledging, even in this tough situation, that God was in control, leaving him with many things for which he could give thanks.

We are given a choice as to how we will view life.
The Bible says: "A man will always reap just the kind
of crop he sows" (Galatians 6:7). You can sow positive
thoughts in your own mind and in the minds of others, or you can sow negative thoughts. Either way, you
reap a harvest.

Your attitude is an important controller in your
life. Proverbs 23:6-8 says: "Don't associate with evil
men; don't long for their favors and gifts. Their kindness is a trick; they want to use you as their pawn. The
delicious food they serve will turn sour in your stom-
ach and you will vomit it, and have to take back your
words of appreciation for their 'kindness.'" Attitudes
select thoughts. Thoughts eventually define who you
are.

Maintaining a good attitude is like weeding a
garden. Constant care is needed. Prayer brings us in
line with God's thoughts. He wants the best for His
children. Confession and repentance cleanse the burdens of past sin. Reading Scripture reaffirms our
positive base. Reading good books further expands
our ability to think positively.

Associate with other positive people who depend on God. Their support will encourage addi-
tional positive attitudes. Your choice of friends is
incredibly important in determining whether or not
you get positive support for your positive thinking.

As a Christian, you can see God working in the
affairs of men from ages past to ages future by reading
from Genesis to Revelation. You can "page forward"
in your own life and see that in the end you are in the
victory circle reigning with Christ.

Since we know the outcome of the affairs of man,

we should be positive. The struggles we go through are for a brief spell, but in the end, a victory celebration awaits us for all eternity.

ON THE PATH TOWARD HONOR

1. Think of an incident in your life that significantly changed your perspective. In what ways has that incident changed your outlook on life? What insights into God's overall plan did you discover?

2. Think back on two situations in the last year where you had a choice of reacting positively or negatively. How did you respond? What do you think would have happened if you had responded differently?

3. Suppose you are surrounded by negative people at work (at school, at home). What are some constructive things you can do to create a positive environment? How will you keep your own attitude positive? Is it possible to change negative people?

2
GOALS

Six Areas Where Clear-Cut Goals Give Meaning to Life

And he will give them to you if you give him first place in your life and live as he wants you to.
(Matthew 6:33)

I strain to reach the end of the race and receive the prize for which God is calling us up to heaven because of what Christ Jesus did for us.
(Philippians 3:14)

Black Beauty, our family's old $100 second car, was crammed full of kids (boy-type) and headed for a special children's gospel meeting at the chapel. The green Mercury was also full of kids (girl-type). Grandma was coming in her own car.

Why all the excitement about gospel meetings? Evangelist Leonard Lindsted had a trunk full of prizes for the kids who brought the most friends. Points were given for bringing adults, kids, your Bible, and for regular attendance. The prizes were big enough to strongly motivate you and your sister Leah into action. (Mom and I had to referee the debate over which one of you got credit for inviting Grandma Oster.)

Clear, visible goals (prizes) were the driving force

21

behind the enthusiasm which filled the chapel with kids. There is something in each one of us which causes us to operate more efficiently when we have goals in mind.

Your goals should reflect God's stated purposes for your life. Here are a few of the major ones:

- to glorify God in all things (1 Corinthians 10:31);
- to minister to others (Romans 14:19);
- to fulfill God-given responsibilities (1 Peter 4:10,11);
- to introduce people to Jesus Christ (2 Peter 3:9);
- to do good works (Titus 3:8);
- to produce spiritual fruit (Colossians 1:10).

Decide what you want to do in each area of your life. Then break the objective down into bite-sized goals, aiming your resources at specific objectives. You'll be surprised how fast you achieve realistic, specific goals. I would encourage goals in at least these six areas.

Spiritual

Every goal area has spiritual implications, but the spiritual goals of your life should be oriented specifically to bringing your life into submission to the Lord's will. Call it Christlikeness, yieldedness, surrender or the Spirit-filled life. It amounts to allowing the self life to give way to the Spirit-guided life.

Goals in this area of your life might center on your desire to exhibit some of the fruits of the Spirit better...to improve your prayer life...to attend seminars with the objective of bringing about a deeper knowledge of God...to read certain books...to read the Bible...to complete a study on some spiritual area.

Since we are called to be disciples, to win others to Christ and to be disciplers for other people, our spiritual goals should include a desire to help others by being an encourager to the Christians around us and by being a witness to those we know who don't have the assurance of eternal life.

Family

Goal-setting in this area might include commitments to spend certain kinds of quality time with each member of the family. Obviously, we hope you will always feel close to your parents and will want to spend time with us.

The most sacred relationship will be with your wife. Your goal-setting process is best completed with common agreement on many areas of your life. Striving toward goals which cause conflict between husband and wife leads to enormous frustration in marriage. Even before you marry, it's a must to discuss some of the major goal areas in both your lives to see if you and your chosen life partner agree on the most basic areas.

Professional

Your job-related goals should include knowing God's will for your vocation. It should include using some of the job-related relationships to win others to Christ. You may want to set out some specific goals relating to improved skills, improved levels of performance and improved financial compensation as a result.

It is good to increase your knowledge in some

area every year through self study. You may have professional seminars, books or other ways of developing new levels of understanding or new skills. You will retrain yourself several times during your career, so be on the alert for new opportunities, even though they may require some specialized training.

One of your goals should be the pursuit of excellence in everything you do on the job. First Corinthians 10:31 urges us, "Well, I'll tell you why. It is because you must do everything for the glory of God, even your eating and drinking."

I know deep down in your heart you want someday to own your own company, or to own a part of it. That requires capital, competence, a reputation which will draw others to you, and some business relationships. Your professional goals should include making some progress each year in one or more areas that will increase your odds of success in the start-up of your own business.

If you prepare yourself, God will give you an opening in due time.

Physical

With the enormous attention given to the physical body these days, you have no shortage of resource material to draw upon. Even though this category of goal-setting says *physical*, there is an important spiritual principle involved in keeping your body fit. In 1 Corinthians 6:19,20 we are reminded, "Haven't you yet learned that your body is the home of the Holy Spirit God gave you, and that he lives within you? Your own body does not belong to you. For God has bought you with a great price. So use every part of your body to give glory back to God, because he owns it."

A good exercise program combined with proper diet will keep you in shape.

Slothfulness in the spiritual area of your life can spill over into the physical area, and vice-versa. If you have unconfessed sin, the weight of guilt can eventually have a depressing impact on your physical being (see Psalm 32:3,4).

Worrying is a threat to good health. Proverbs 17:22 reminds us, "A cheerful heart does good like medicine, but a broken spirit makes one sick."

Disobedience is another health threat. Proverbs 4:20-22 reminds us, "Listen, son of mine, to what I say. Listen carefully. Keep these thoughts ever in mind; let them penetrate deep within your heart, for they will mean real life for you, and radiant health."

Mental

Over a period of time we tend to become the person whom our thoughts tell us we are. In a world filled with so much negative impact through music, television, motion pictures and the print media, we must carefully select those mental inputs which are worthy of our attention.

Quality music, quality motion pictures, quality art, quality theater, and quality books — especially the Bible — are positive inputs.

Challenge your mind by reading at least one or two books each month. Keep up your reading speed to college level or improve it to 1,000 words a minute if you can. Read newspapers, magazines and Christian periodicals so you can discern the new ways Satan is attacking God's people.

Your prayer and meditation play a key role in determining the quality of what you keep in your mind. Dwell on the pure things of life and on eternity.

Social

The friends you keep and the conversations you carry on with them have a great impact on your mind. Maintain contact with some of the really bright people you have met. They will continually be a challenge to you if their goals are God-directed.

Your goals in this area should include the cultivation of friends who can minister to your needs, and some to whom you can minister. A good balance of each keeps you from living an imbalanced social life. Constantly feeding others without refueling yourself will drain you. Or, on the other extreme, if you are constantly being fed by someone else without using that information to help another person, you stagnate as a Christian.

The blessings God gives you, including your friendships, prepare you to give something to others who need you.

The cycle of good social relationships begins with you. To find a friend, you must first be a friend.

Your social goals should include finding new friends each year: some more mature who can encourage you, some less mature whom you can help along in the Christian life through your fellowship.

Personal

I have seen you write out goals in this area of your life, so you are already ahead of most people your age.

Achievement of worthy goals is the definition of success. Achievement of goals in only one or two areas, however, results in narrowness or imbalance.

Goal-setting is critical to making progress in our lives. If you don't define where you want to go, your life won't be lived with direction or order.

If over a long period you feel that you aren't achieving any goals, you can be a candidate for "burn-out" — a depressing feeling that you are working hard without achieving anything important. Literally millions of people are receiving psychological counsel for depression, deep discouragement and other maladies which might have been averted with clear-cut goals.

Goals are the check points on the journey to a full life. They are the finish lines of our dreams. A clear set of goals gives you an opportunity to check off specific accomplishments as they are completed, giving you a sense of achievement. Without such a list, your failure in one area can pull you down because you failed to give yourself credit for achieving goals in several other areas of your life. Each long-range goal should be reviewed and updated at least once a year.

Goals become the criteria for decision making. Some goals are big and life-long. The apostle Paul said, "I press toward the mark of the high calling of God in Christ Jesus." Paul made pleasing God his number one goal. That goal influenced his priorities, his friendships and his conversation. It even influenced his attitude toward his captors when he was in prison.

Goals keep us moving in a consistent direction. They give meaning to our lives.

Perhaps the biggest value of goal-setting is that it keeps us focused on the future. Paul said, "No, dear brothers, I am still not all I should be but I am bringing all my energies to bear on this one thing: Forgetting the past and looking forward to what lies ahead, I strain to reach the end of the race and receive the prize for which God is calling us up to Heaven because of what Christ Jesus did for us" (Philippians 3:13,14).

Goals keep you focused on results. Results are more important than activity. The activity of our lives should be aimed at getting specific results.

You Can't Hit a Target Without Aiming

In a world that can absorb all the time you can spare, there is great danger in focusing on activity instead of results. A good way to stop this drift: At the end of a week or a month, take a fresh look at your goals. Then review the daily list of things which occupied most of your time. If the bulk of your activity wasn't directly related to your goals, then you may have to refocus your activity. You may be doing things right, but still burn out because you're not doing the right things.

Being accountable for hours invested in achieving goals gently trains us to become disciplined. Discipline might be defined as clearly understanding our goals, then accomplishing them, regardless of the circumstances.

As you crystalize the list of goals in your mind, you find the courage to say no to things which clearly don't line up with the direction you believe God is leading you.

Time management is much easier when you keep

your goals ever in front of you. Some things clearly take higher priority than others because of your stated goals.

Jesus left us with a good example. He came to do His Father's will. When in Mark 1:32-38 the disciples found Jesus they said, "Everyone is looking for you." Why *wouldn't* they be looking for the one who was healing the sick and casting out demons? Jesus replied to the disciples, "Let us go somewhere else — to the nearby villages — so I can preach there also. That is why I have come."

Our Lord could have filled His day with healing (which would have amazed thousands), but He focused His limited time on earth on those things which led directly toward His goal.

Your grandfather knew how to lighten the burden of a hard-working day by setting some goals. One of his goals was to replace a muddy barnyard with a concrete floor. But he converted the big goal into little objectives that my brother Larry and I could understand. Dad announced that we were going to borrow a cement mixer and each day pour a six-foot-wide strip across the cow yard until we had it done.

Cement work is hard work. It means shoveling a ton or more of sand and cement into a mixer by hand each day, pushing it across the yard in a wheelbarrow, striking it off with a two-by-four board, then troweling it smooth. After the first day, under a hot sun, we were just about dead.

The next morning Dad said, "Boys, when we get the strip done today, we're going to head to Waterloo for a swim in the Byrnes Park pool."

Now, with a goal in mind, the sand shovel seemed

to weigh only half as much. The work was bearable. We finished that strip an hour earlier, in great anticipation that the heat of the day would be broken by the cool water of the pool.

Dad's goal was to get the cows out of the mud. But he gave your Uncle Larry and me a goal we could realize immediately — going swimming. That is a bit of management psychology Dad taught me in the barnyard. I pass it on to you.

Our nation was built by men who ate only if they worked. One of the challenges we face today is that we are breeding an "entitlement" generation that doesn't see the necessary connection between work and rewards. If American leadership is to stop this cancer, you and I must do what we can to preserve the lesson of setting goals and receiving positive rewards.

ON THE PATH TOWARD HONOR

1. On a separate piece of paper, list your specific goals for the next five years in each of these areas:

Spiritual   Family   Professional   Personal

Physical   Mental   Social

2. Break down your long-range goals in each of these areas into a succession of short-range goals which work toward the five-year mark. During the next two weeks place your short-range goals on a timetable, starting with this month. Where do you need to be six months from now? A year from now? Two years from now? Three and four years from now?

3. What specific tasks will you need to undertake *this week* in order to begin to reach your stated goals?

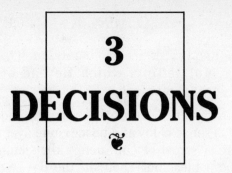

3
DECISIONS
❦

Five Guidelines for Making Hard Choices

Without wise leadership, a nation is in trouble; but with good counselors there is safety.

(Proverbs 11:14)

I slipped out just after dawn, quietly walking down the stairs of the farm house, across the yard, past the barn and out to the gravel road. There I began to pray out loud.

The decision at hand was whether or not to leave a stable job so we could return to Iowa and strike out on our own. It was spring, 1969. Your mom and I had weighed the pros and cons and had been praying about the move.

The smells and sounds of spring surrounded me as I sought God's will for a career change and a move. I came to the top of the hill and stopped where the slight elevation opened up a view of the whole farm. I felt as though I could reach out and touch the Lord in this peaceful setting, which He had created, it seemed, for this moment.

On the way down the hill, as I continued to talk to the Lord, a sense of joy and peace came over me. I was bathed in a sense of confidence that such a move would be a blessing. Then, in the days which followed, I looked for confirming pieces of evidence. Nearly every light turned green.

I received confirming encouragement on the move to Iowa from men at Downing Avenue Gospel Chapel. Bill Ramsey took me on Sunday afternoon evangelistic calls even before we moved, encouraging me to get involved with the local church. Wendell Lockard once said, "Move back here and we'll do something special together for the Lord." We have since been a blessing to each other.

Before we made the move, though, there was one more test. Could my decision be swayed by economics? When I walked into the boss's office to announce I was leaving, he gave me a strong pitch to stay. He said, "Think about it and we'll talk on Monday."

On Monday, he asked if a raise from my $13,000 salary to $20,000 would keep me on the job. I said, "No." Two or three days later he told me how much he and the owner appreciated my efforts and asked if a $30,000 salary would change my mind. I said, "No amount of money would change my mind because it is a decision based on bigger issues than money." That was a step of faith.

Once we got our direction, your mom and I didn't announce it to the world. Instead, we began to work toward our goal, and informed people of our plans on

a "need to know" basis. The decision was welcomed
by almost everyone; however, our many friends at the
Lake Geneva Bible Chapel in nearby Lake Geneva,
Wisconsin, were sorry to see us go.

We made the move in October of 1969. You were
five; Leah was three.

With a 10-foot by 30-foot office and a part-time
secretary, we opened a new business. Several clients
provided work in the communications area. Each afternoon I headed out to the farm. The Lord never gave
me clear direction on whether I was to be a farmer or a
journalist, so I did both.

God had spoken. I had listened. That decision
was to change hundreds of lives and influence thousands as it opened the way for further blessings that
included the development of Professional Farmers of
America, *Futures* magazine, Oster Communications
and other businesses God has led us to develop over
the years. God's blessings went way beyond anything
we ever expected.

Our most immediate blessing, though, was that as
a family we moved close to your Grandpa and Grandma Oster, just months before he was stricken with
cancer. You and Leah got some very special attention
that only a grandpa can give. I had the opportunity to
farm next to my dad for a year. I was home to pick up
the pieces when he couldn't farm for himself any-
more. We decided he would call the shots from the
house and I would do the farming. Grandpa didn't
live to see that harvest, but he was around long
enough to plant some important seeds in your life.

Had we lacked the courage or faith to step out, we
would have missed out on two wonderful years in

Grandpa's life.

The Art of Making Wise Decisions

I have seen God's hand clearly in many other decisions. Your mom and I were led to each other after years of prayer that God would send the right person into our lives. The start-up of Professional Farmers of America was only after seeing the Lord open some doors. Many specific smaller decisions, including my entry into journalism, were made after being led by a sense of peace following a period of prayer.

Unfortunately, at times I have stepped out on my own without seeking God's will and have made some glaring errors by running off in my own direction. So let me sum up for you some of the guidelines I try to use when making hard choices.

1. Bathe the issue in prayer.

2. Seek out the advice of godly men.

3. Gather all the information available, biblical and secular, that has a bearing on the decision.

4. Look for openings — little signs that God is leading in one direction or another.

5. Wait for all of the above to be pulled together by the Holy Spirit into a "sense of peace" about the issue.

When we returned to Iowa, within a few miles of the home farm, it was in hopes that you and your sister would be able to enjoy the same surroundings where I was taught some practical lessons about life. Many of my decision-making lessons were learned in the barn. Let me take you on a little tour.

Slide the door to your right and step into the cow

barn. Twenty-six stanchions. Twenty-six cows to milk when every stanchion is full.

Along this aisle, there are calf pens on the right. Pens that need regular cleaning. Let's pause here at the gate to the last pen.

One evening after school, when I was fourteen, I was right here with orders from Dad to help pitch manure out of that pen. Testing my new-found manhood as a fourteen-year-old, I told Dad in a condescending voice, "Why do you want to waste our time cleaning this pen today? It doesn't need it." Without any anger Dad said, "This pen does need cleaning. Two of us can do it in fifteen minutes, or I can do it alone in thirty."

My rebellious attitude collapsed. In a few words Dad said so much. He, in effect, told me I had a choice: go my own rebellious way or follow his leadership. He instinctively knew when it was time to quit telling a boy what to do and begin making him responsible for his own decisions.

He gave me the freedom to make that choice, even if it meant a personal sacrifice.

He had also told me I was a man, because with my help he could get the job done twice as fast.

The pen was clean in fifteen minutes!

There's no class on decision-making that will ever compare with the classroom of the calf pen.

That same calf pen later housed my purebred Holstein heifer calf. I had wanted to be in 4-H, and Dad suggested buying a dairy heifer. "Herman Hemingway has a good purebred herd, only a mile north on the gravel road," he said. "Talk to Herman and pick your own calf." I talked with Herman. He gave me my pick of the pen for $100.

The next summer at the county fair I stood at the extreme end of the line in the Holstein heifer class — the wrong end. I took home the last white ribbon they passed out. I was mad. Mad at Dad? No. Mad at Herman? No. I was reaping the harvest of my own choice of calves.

The next month I announced I'd like to get into the hog business. Dad said, "Fine. Next time I go to Dike, I'll drop you off at Louie Jorgensen's and you can try to buy a couple of gilts. He has some good meaty pigs."

I spent two hours looking over Louie's hogs. I had a short stick in one hand and a small pail of grease in the other. When I found a gilt I liked, I slapped some grease on her back.

But on this selection trip, I was armed with a bulletin from the Extension Service and some experience gained by training for the county livestock judging team. I made my choices. Three white gilts.

For the next three summers I showed the grand champion litter, pen-of-three and individual market hogs at the Butler County Fair. Again, I was reaping the harvest of my own decisions, a process that started in that calf pen.

The move to Iowa achieved our objectives. Within a few years, that same calf pen where I used to keep my calves was filled with your 4-H project steers. There you learned to work, to follow instructions, to make choices, to enjoy the many benefits of rural life.

It's amazing how good decisions made early in

life tend to have a multiplicative effect. Don't forget that the Lord is an integral part of your decision-making team only if you invite Him, in prayer, to give you direction.

ON THE PATH TOWARD HONOR

1. Think about a major decision you'll be making within the next six months. Have you asked God for guidance? Who will you seek out for advice? Where will you find the information you'll need to make a wise decision? What are some of the "green lights" you'll be looking for?

2. How does your freedom of choice affect your decision-making process?

3. Think of a wise decision you have made in the past. What were the results? How are you benefiting from that decision now?

4
ACCOUNTABILITY

❧

What Answering to Authority Accomplishes

Yes, each of us will give an account of himself to God.

(Romans 14:12)

I walked half fearful into the room filled with active members of FarmHouse fraternity at Iowa State University. This was my hour for "criticism" by the active members. If I responded to their critique and kept up my grades, then one day I would be an active member.

One by one they dressed me down, built me up, peppered questions. I left feeling like a misfit.

"Oster, that dangling New Hartford Hawk sign on your back bumper has to go. You're a college man now," one man charged.

"When you talk to people, look them squarely in the eye," said another. "You're pretty cocky for a first

41

quarter freshman. How many hours do you study each week? That's what counts at FarmHouse."

The first session was intended to be brutal on the freshmen. Maybe they were a bit tougher on me because they recruited me directly out of high school, the first person to be so "honored."

But as the months went by and the critique sessions became more positive, men one to four years older than I reviewed my social and academic performance. They found my strong points and encouraged me to develop them. They spotted my faults and suggested ways I could improve.

Within that group there were some special men: Jerry Carlson, my pledge father, with whom I have worked daily for the past fourteen years; Jim Frevert, my first roommate, who stops in almost every year to keep our friendship fresh.

The point is this: When I was at home, I was accountable to my father and mother. In college I was accountable to my fraternity brothers, university instructors and several employers.

As an adult I have felt an accountability to your mom, Ray Routley, Dan Dunnett, and other church leaders and business associates. From time to time I have felt accountable to friends — people who cared for me enough to advise, encourage, warn. You need such a group.

Find a good church and put yourself under its authority. Find some men a few years older than yourself who will be "spiritual mentors."

Feeling the need for such an accountability group, I recently called a breakfast meeting chaired by

Jerry Carlson. A group of men who have exhibited a long history of caring for me reviewed my strengths and warned me about the pitfalls that go with those strengths. They offered words of encouragement, correction and direction.

I have been reminded that not one of us is a "Lone Ranger." We influence the lives of many other people and have a responsibility to God for the way we invest our time, money and talent. The wise counsel of other men, and the feeling of being accountable to them, creates positive changes in our lives.

ON THE PATH TOWARD HONOR

1. To whom are you accountable at this point in your life? In what ways have these people developed your character? What wise counsel have you received over the past three months?

2. Think of one person who has had a great influence in your life because of his or her encouragement and caring confrontations. Why did you listen to this person? What did you learn about yourself? Whose life are you influencing right now?

5
TEACHABILITY

Stimulating an Appetite for Learning

The man who knows right from wrong and has good judgment and common sense is happier than the man who is immensely rich! For such wisdom is far more valuable than precious jewels.

(Proverbs 3:13,14)

As we stand at the east barn door on our farm, you'll notice the contours on that field across the road. Those contours tell a story about your grandpa.

In one of my early years of 4-H, when I was either fourteen or fifteen, I decided to give a demonstration on the importance of contour farming. This type of farming reduces pollution by controlling field water runoff. I built a box for a model contour hill, collected the information and practiced my demonstration. I won the county contest and became quite overconfident as I headed to the Iowa State Fair for higher competition. In fact, I hardly practiced for the State Fair because I thought I was pretty good.

I learned for the first time what it is like to go flat

in front of an audience.

I tasted the "agony of defeat" in the form of a white ribbon, the lowest of three categories they awarded. Did I learn a lesson from that trip!

On an April afternoon the following spring I looked out the school bus window as we approached the farm to see a grader, a tractor and a plow working the hill just southeast of the barn.

I jumped out of the bus, changed my pants in thirty-five seconds flat (leaving my usual path of strewn school clothes and books), and headed to the field.

To my amazement, Dad and the man from the Grundy County Soil Conservation Service were laying out a contour! I saw in my dad a quality that graduate schools of business have a hard time teaching. It's the ability to learn from others and to apply that knowledge profitably. Dad had heard the facts through the mouth of a teenage son and wasn't too proud to implement his son's ideas.

The ability to learn from someone else. Dad gave me a graphic demonstration of that ability right there on that hill.

There is a wonderful training scene in Scripture. The Lord is walking with His disciples on the road near Emmaus. Scripture tells us that He explained the Bible as they went. Maybe that's when the disciples got the "big picture" of the eternal view of man from God's perspective. What a privilege to be taught by the creator of the universe!

Yet, we have a similar privilege, if we are teachable. As Christians we have the Holy Spirit within us to teach. We also have able people around us to teach. The opportunity is much broader than the church service. All across America there are Bible studies among businessmen where one is teaching another.

As you look southeast from that old barn today, you see our new home. In a way, it stands as a monument to all those lessons I learned on the farm and passed along to you and your sister.

When we built the house, it happened to lie across the top of that contour which Dad had built nearly twenty years earlier. After the contractors completed the house, I had the landscapers rebuild the contour right up to the edge of the lawn.

You may wonder why I took so much time personally shoveling that soil back and raking it down myself. Well, part of the reason is that I didn't want the water from the house yard to run over the corn field. But the real reason is that I wanted to preserve the contour, to preserve an important lesson of life built into it by a previous generation.

Don't Depend on "Spoon-Feeding"

A county soil judging contest was scheduled for the county seat town of Allison on a school day. By entering the contest, I could be excused from school. So I entered.

Unlike the students who had vocational agriculture teachers to train them on soil judging, I came from New Hartford where there was no such teacher. I ordered the book the other fellows had in their classroom and still remember studying while lying on my tummy in front of the bedroom window overlooking the wash house and chicken house to the south.

For two or three hours at a time, on two or three occasions, I studied the book so I wouldn't look stupid at the contest. At the contest I did just what the book said to do. Pinch the soil, see if it made a ribbon or if it had grains of sand as you pinched it between the fingers.

I handed in my sheet. The scores were tallied. I won. I was shocked. Book learning had won over classroom "spoon-feeding."

That experience gave me great appreciation for self study. Since that high school day, I have picked up knowledge on managing an organization, futures trading, direct mail and many other areas . . . by reading books.

I've seen you tackle stamp collecting, technical analysis of futures, rock collecting and other areas with the same enthusiasm. You've already learned a great lesson — that you don't have to be spoon-fed in a classroom to learn a new skill.

With that confidence, develop one area of your knowledge so thoroughly that you are the very best. Know all of the good authors, all of the successful practitioners of whatever area you choose. In the early stages of your career, you may want to focus on some area of your profession. Also focus on an area of Bible knowledge and a hobby.

Master some body of knowledge. It will make you an interesting person.

At the same time, keep your radar set at a wide angle. I do that by reading a newspaper from both coasts regularly. You get a different perspective on the nation. Read at least one magazine which has a foreign flavor — to get a world view. Read Christian periodicals.

Build your library with quality books. You may
be sick of books for a while after you leave college, but
never walk by a bookstore without looking at one or
two flyleaves. That's a way to increase your appetite
for learning something.

There also must be an inner desire and a love for
what you are doing. As we stand here in the east barn
door, I remember a lesson along that line. You can see
right over there where the feed bunk used to stand.
Dad used to pull the flare box wagon loaded with
ground corn through the gate and park it at the head of
the row of three lined-up feed bunks. He would scoop
a bushel basket full of corn, then start pouring it at the
far end of the third bunk. I never saw him hurry. He
would pause, look over the cattle, get another basket
and deliberately walk back down the bunk, carefully
glancing from side to side — I suppose checking to see
if there was a lame foot or a runny nose in the bunch.

As I used to lean on the barn door waiting for a
cow to be milked, I'd watch him. Something about the
way he did things said to me that he loved what he was
doing. He had a burning desire to see a job done
thoroughly.

I never recall him telling me, "Son, one of the
secrets of success is burning desire. You've got to
develop a burning desire — a deep love for what you
want to accomplish in life." No, he never told me to
have burning desire. He just lived it, every day.

Sometimes our actions say much more than an
hour of lecture. There's no classroom that can instill a
burning desire for accomplishment. I believe the
seeds for those thoughts are planted in our homes, or

in the barn.

There were many learning opportunities on the farm. I could tell you about the basketball court at one end of the haymow. I probably should hate haymows today after the many thousands of bales I stacked there on 90-degree days. But we always emptied the south end of the haymow first because there were baskets on the east and west side of that end. It was always nice to take a chore break and play a quick game of basketball. That's where Dad taught me about balancing my life between work and play. Not with a lecture, but by taking a break and playing.

There's much more to this campus in the barn-yard of rural America. There were the lessons in frugality taught in the well house, which also served as a shop. Of course, the important business and economic lesson of "don't put all your eggs in one basket" could only be learned in the hen house. I could take you to the kitchen table where the whole superstructure for my value system was formed, not so much by lectures on what was good and what was bad, but by listening to the conversation and perceiving what was good and what was bad based on judgments and observations made by my parents.

I could show you the stair steps up to my bedroom. On the only day I ever played hookey from school, I came home that night, headed past the kitchen table and up the stairs two steps at a time, to avoid my mom. Mom took one step at a time, but twice as fast.

Once again, I had made a choice. As I looked over my shoulder at the top of the stairs I could tell by the fire in her eyes that I was about to pay the price for making a wrong choice. Some lessons must be taught with a paddle in hand! As the recipient of a few of my paddlings, you know how well I learned that lesson and passed it on to you.

Be teachable. You'll grow in many ways, much faster than those who think they know it all.

ON THE PATH TOWARD HONOR

1. Think of one or two things you have learned by observing your parents. How have you applied that knowledge profitably in your life? How do you plan to share this knowledge with the next generation?

2. What area of knowledge or new skill interests you? Over the next two weeks plan and implement a course of self study in this area. (Start with a trip to your local library.)

3. Are you open to the lessons that God has for you in the various circumstances of your life? What have you learned in the past month from those around you? What can you learn from the experience and role-modeling of your colleagues and friends? Do you have a teachable spirit?

6
CRISES

Benefits of Trials

*God is our refuge and strength, a tested help in
times of trouble.*

(Psalm 46:1)

*These troubles and sufferings of ours are, after all,
quite small and won't last very long. Yet this short
time of distress will result in God's richest blessing
upon us forever and ever.*

(2 Corinthians 4:17)

As a twelve-year-old, you rolled the lawn
mower over into an eight-foot ditch. We were headed
to Grandma's with two lawn mowers so we could
finish quickly. Somehow, your lawn mower jumped
off the road, rolled completely over in the ditch and
righted itself without scratching you.

God's protective hand was on you that day! But I
should have taken the hint that this wouldn't be your
last crisis.

When you were in high school, a telephone call to
my office one fall afternoon informed me that you and
Leah had been in an accident and had been hauled
away in an ambulance. No one knew how badly you

were hurt.

The two-minute trip to the hospital emergency room got me there just as they were opening the ambulance doors. When I saw your troubled faces, I was immediately relieved that you were both alive. Looking at the pickup later that evening, I stood in tears praising God for sparing your lives. Again, His hand was on you in a mighty way.

Most of life's crises aren't life-threatening, but they can be ego-damaging, discouraging and difficult in many ways.

For self-confident persons like you and me, God frequently uses crisis situations which are out of our control to teach us that we must depend on Him.

How we respond to crisis is the *real* test of our character. The Bible tells us to count it all joy when troubles mount, because it is evidence that God is at work in our lives. It takes a mature Christian to see trouble from that point of view. That's why moving toward Christian maturity is so important. It prepares us to handle the next level of crisis.

Some crises leave you feeling alone, as though no one in the world cares whether you live or die. Of course, that is never true — but sometimes Satan tempts us to believe it.

In those times of loneliness, we learn to cast ourselves upon the Lord, for He is always there. Always with us. Always available to guide us through the deep waters. Sometimes we pray for Him to remove the crisis, but real growth usually is a result of working through the crisis with God's help.

It has been my experience that during such dark

days, Bible verses I have read many times before suddenly shine with new light. They take on a deeper meaning. They provide promise. They encourage. They direct. They correct. They give hope of a fresh start. They assure me of total forgiveness, if that's what's needed.

Sometimes a crisis just slows us down. "Be still and know that I am God," says the psalmist.

Sometimes trials come in the form of boring repetition...the same routine day after day after day. Such was the case with the wandering Hebrews in Exodus 16:35. God gave them manna. Every day. Fresh manna. Manna sandwiches. Boiled manna. Baked manna. Hot manna. Cold manna. Raw manna. Cooked manna.

Why such a boring diet? The answer is in Exodus 16:4: "The Lord said to Moses, 'Look, I'm going to rain down food from heaven for them. Everyone can go out each day and gather as much food as he needs. And I will test them in this, to see whether they will follow my instructions or not.'"

Those trials that hang on, sometimes for years, are character-building opportunities. Our attitude should be, "What can I learn from this test?"

The Thrill of Victory

As an amateur marathon runner, I have a real appreciation for the way the professionals prepare for a 26.2-mile race. Marathon runners prepare their bodies by gradually increasing their training runs. From 4-mile runs, to 6 miles, 8 miles, 12 miles and finally an occasional 20- to 22-mile training run.

Each new increment in the training process

moves the runner closer to his goal — being able to endure the full 26.2-mile marathon run. At each higher level of fitness, a runner plateaus for a few days or weeks before tackling the bigger challenge of the next longer distance.

Perhaps James had the marathon runner in mind when he wrote: "Dear brothers, is your life full of difficulties and temptations? Then be happy, for when the way is rough, your patience has a chance to grow" (James 1:2,3).

Trials produce endurance. Endurance is necessary for completing the race. Completion, not winning, is the objective of most marathon runners. But victory, not just finishing, is the *guarantee* of the Christian. Our victory was accomplished at the cross. There Jesus died and rose victorious over sin, death and hell.

Since victory is assured to all who put their trust in Christ, the trials we face are indications that God is at work in our lives. He is increasing our level of endurance so we can do more good for the kingdom by carrying heavier burdens in the future.

In James 1:12, the writer spells out victory: "Happy is the man who doesn't give in and do wrong when he is tempted, for afterwards he will get as his reward the crown of life that God has promised those who love him."

Although there are many trials which provide endurance to be used in earthly experiences, we can be assured that trials ultimately result in eternal rewards for those who persevere.

The next trial which you will undergo, whatever it is, will produce endurance. Your roots will grow deeper so you can stand stronger winds. God is producing big timber — you!

ON THE PATH TOWARD HONOR

1. Think of a crisis that you have faced during the past year. Was it life-threatening? Ego-damaging? Discouraging? What was your response at the time of the crisis? How do you view that crisis now?

2. God uses the crises in our lives for character-building opportunities. List some valuable lessons you have learned from the "deep waters" in your life. In what ways does this help you face the next crisis you'll encounter?

7

PREPAREDNESS

❦

The Importance of Being Ready for Eternity

And just as it is destined that men die only once, and after that comes judgment, so also Christ died only once as an offering for the sins of many people; and he will come again, but not to deal again with our sins. This time he will come bringing salvation to all those who are eagerly and patiently waiting for him.

(Hebrews 9:27,28)

Let me take you back to the farm again for a little lesson I picked up there. We'll go to the new room built onto the front of the old farmhouse.

Dad was physically exhausted and lying on the couch. The laboratory report was in. I had already told Mother the bad news. Our family had always met difficult situations head-on so we could deal with crisis in the light of day. "It's cancer, Dad," I said. "The fast kind. Now, there are several things the doctors want to do, and we've got to start tomorrow..."

Dad said nothing, just nodded his head in acceptance.

No eloquent speech on hope, no sermon on faith

59

could ever say more to me than that accepting nod of his head. It was the clincher. It told me in a new and practical way that when faced with life's ultimate challenge, faith works. Your grandpa was prepared to die because more than twenty years earlier he had accepted Jesus Christ as his own Savior and Lord.

Within six months of that day on the porch, we all stood around his hospital bed, knowing that the end of Dad's earthly journey was near. He asked to see you and Leah, his only grandchildren. The following day your grandpa passed away.

I was not prepared for the days that followed. Tributes came from every corner of our rural community. A truck driver for the New Hartford Elevator summed up the comments of many people. Choked up as he stood with the family at the funeral home, he said, "He was a good man."

A neighboring farmer walked up to me near the casket and said, "You have big shoes to fill." In an instant I realized that all the honors I had won as a high school and college student and all my professional accomplishments didn't amount to much. They added up to *what I had done*. This man knew Dad for *who he was*.

Your grandpa was well liked because he spoke kindly of others, had a quiet sense of humor, preferred a second place for himself and was an encourager of other people. No wonder the funeral procession was more than a mile long. Dad left his mark on many people. Mom, as a schoolteacher, also left her influence on many of them.

Our lives should be lived with the view of "Am I ready? Will anyone care if I'm gone?"

I wrote a little tract, which we passed out at the funeral, titled, "Don't Wait Too Long." It was based on a statement Dad made to a relative who wasn't ready when he visited Dad's bedside in those final weeks:

> As a friend of Dad's you should know the only request he made on his death bed. A visitor was at his bedside. The conversation was about eternal matters. Dad assured his visitor that he had God's promise of eternal life in heaven. On March 18, 1949, he had put his faith in the Lord Jesus Christ as Savior.
>
> So it was, with deep-seated confidence of his own salvation and concern over an unsaved friend, he looked up from his bed and made this request, "DON'T WAIT TOO LONG."
>
> If you have not yet made your peace with God by putting your trust in the finished work of the cross, you would do well to let the words of this request ring in your heart until you find true peace.

That inward peace Dad knew was proven to us time and again during his illness. It was quite evident that he knew the "peace of God which passeth understanding." It was first revealed when Dad accepted the news that he had cancer without flinching a muscle or uttering a word.

He had early hope that some miracle drug would pull him through. But that hope was dashed when his appetite failed. Although disappointed, Dad was comforted by the fact that this was part of God's plan. "There's a purpose in all things," he told a visitor.

For several weeks Dad must have been torn between the desire to be relieved of his pain and be forever with the Lord, and the desire to be with those of us he loved. I will never forget the moments he spent with his five- and seven-year-old grandchildren as they held his hands. How he looked forward to watching them grow up. The children understood in their own ways that their "Poppie" would not recover. What a disappointment it must have been to Dad to look into their sad eyes, knowing he would have to leave them soon, and to leave his life-long partner who so faithfully stood by his side in all of life.

Yet, because he saw life in its true perspective of eternity, leaving loved ones was a disappointment he could bear.

Then, in those final days when pain could not be eased by drugs, he refused to complain. He had the assurance of God's Word that God would not allow any more suffering than he could endure.

The purpose in passing these thoughts along is not to call attention to my father, because he was not the kind of man who would seek attention, but to call attention to the one Dad knew, and the one he would like you to know — the Lord Jesus Christ.

When he asked the visitor not to wait too long, he was referring to the all-important decision each one of us must make for eternity: "What will you do with Christ?"

Dad understood from the Bible that man, by his nature, is in rebellion against God. Man must be born again and restored into fellowship with God through faith in Jesus Christ who paid the penalty for man's sins through His death (John 3:3). Man receives, when he trusts Christ, the gift of eternal life and will enjoy the pleasure of living with God for all eternity (John 3:16).

Dad's request is an urgent one because of the uncertainty of life, and because those who fail to ask forgiveness for their sins and put their faith in the Lord Jesus Christ, will, after death, be raised for judgment and will suffer eternal punishment (John 3:18).

If you yearn for real peace, deep peace, you can find it through a personal knowledge of the Lord Jesus Christ as your Savior. If Dad could, he would urge you to trust Him today. And when you trust Christ, tell someone about it so the new life in you can shine out to others.

Then in that soon-coming day all of us who know Christ as Savior will be reunited with our loved ones. We will be with Dad again — precious thought. But more than that, we will enjoy true peace in the presence of our Lord Jesus Christ.

Dave, I know you are ready, but the Lord will put in your path many who aren't. Look for opportunities to <u>be a beacon</u> for those still on the wrong path, without Christ.

And I'd suggest you read Marilyn Heavilin's comments on "Troubles, Traumas and Trials" in the companion book *Mother to Daughter: Becoming a Woman of Honor.* Marilyn has faced death in her immediate family on several occasions with the result being a deepening of her dependence on God.

ON THE PATH TOWARD HONOR

1. Think through your life up to this point. If you were to die tonight, would you be remembered for what you had done or for who you were? How would you like to be remembered?

2. Are you ready? How have you prepared yourself for eternity?

3. List the friends God has put in your path who are not prepared for death. What are some practical ways you can point them to the one who has conquered death?

8
MONEY

Six Principles For Managing Money Wisely

The Lord's blessing is our greatest wealth. All our work adds nothing to it.

(Proverbs 10:22)

Always remember that it is the Lord your God who gives you power to become rich, and he does it to fulfill his promise to your ancestors.

(Deuteronomy 8:18)

The Professional Farmers of America seminar was called to order, and I introduced Jim Gill as the speaker on market timing. To my surprise, you were in the front row taking notes. You were nine years old!

To everyone else's surprise, you were still there at coffee break time.

With great relief, I saw you jump into the pool with the other kids early in the afternoon.

A few weeks later, you and I walked onto the trading floor of the MidAmerica Commodity Exchange after trading had closed. You picked up some cards off the floor and began jotting down silver price quotes. Bob Collins, president of the MidAmerica

Commodity Exchange, was so impressed with your conversation that he said, "This is no kid. He must be a midget."

You have had a keen interest in money and the various futures instruments for a long time. That interest has led you to think globally about the events that influence prices of silver, gold, stock indexes, and others. Your interest in trading sharpened your interest in world politics and world trade. You're now headed for a job on Wall Street, a result of your early understanding of how financial-laden information moves futures prices. That New York trading desk job you lined up is quite a leap from rural Iowa. Congratulations!

A word of caution is in order. You will be around "big money" in New York. Money is power in this world, so be careful how you think about it.

Money isn't neutral. It tends to be used either as a powerful tool for investment in God's works, or as an all-consuming worldly taskmaster.

Your attitude toward money will determine whether it is a positive or negative force in your life. If you accumulate money for materialistic or selfish goals, it will destroy. But by accumulating and managing money wisely to be reinvested, or given back to God, you play a critical role in building the kingdom. You will be blessed, and blessed abundantly.

Here are a few biblical principles — so simple yet so profound — which I have found helpful in gaining a proper perspective on money.

1. God Owns It All

If we really believe God owns everything, we take

a different approach to life and possessions. If God owns everything, I am a steward — someone managing God's property temporarily. With that attitude toward our home, car, money and other possessions, we become a more sharing kind of people. We seek out ways to use these resources to benefit their real owner, the Lord.

Here's a job description that applies to all Christians who want to act as responsible stewards. You can personalize it by adding a specific list of ways you believe God is directing you to utilize your unique mix of time, talent, gifts and earthly treasures which He has entrusted to you for a few years of management.

JOB DESCRIPTION

STEWARD: TRUSTEE OF GOD'S RESOURCES

Mission: To glorify God by managing everything God entrusts to me in a way that adds people into His kingdom (evangelism) and encourages those already in the kingdom (discipleship).

Key Functions:

1. Follow Christ. Allow God's character, love and purpose to flow through me in a way that impacts others.

2. Appropriate His power. By yielding to God's control, allow the Holy Spirit to direct and empower each activity.

3. Tell others. Reproduce His life in the lives of others.

4. Manage my self. Manage my time, talent, gifts and treasures to maximize the advancement of the cause of Christ.

Key Results:

1. See Christ live through me in a way that leads others

to Him.

2. Bring encouragement to others in the body of Christ.

3. Live a life of peace, purpose and significance knowing I am part of a great plan.

Reporting Responsibility:

1. Report to my heavenly Father.

2. Submit to the authority of the local church.

3. Submit to world authority.

4. Work in submissive harmony with other stewards.

Spheres of Influence:

1. Self

2. Family

3. Friends and neighbors

4. Business associates

5. Community

6. Local church

7. State, nation, world

2. You Can't Take It With You

Besides a knowledge of God's Word, the only
thing in life we can take with us is people. Men and
women we influence to become members of the kingdom will be part of the greeting party in heaven.

We can "send money ahead" by our stewardship
decisions here, but we can't take it with us.

3. Giving While We're Living Yields a Big Return

Giving while we're living not only provides more
joy and satisfaction, but it's also a way to achieve

eternal investment objectives which, according to Scripture, yield a 10,000 percent (hundredfold) return.

If we view ourselves as channels through which God can entrust resources to be managed for His kingdom, we gain the proper perspective on life. An objective of piling up the biggest fortune for the sake of "winning" is selfish, and has no real end, so it can have no lasting satisfaction for the "hoarder."

However, the reasonable accumulation of capital through savings or earnings of a company provides a base from which to live and give. The Bible says little against possessing wealth. It is the worship of wealth (wealth possessing you) which Scripture warns against.

There are tremendous needs in the world which will be met by generous wealthy men and women who have a vision to use their blessings. There is a biblical principle behind their expecting further blessings when they manage their wealth with the proper attitude.

4. There's Incredible Power in Compound Interest

This is the most important piece of money management information you can get. It wasn't until I was twenty-four that the real impact of compounding hit me. Here's the story.

If you can accumulate $10,000 in a savings account in the next four years and then let it grow at a 10 percent interest rate without any further additions for the next forty years, it will be worth $450,000; $2.7 million at a 15 percent growth rate; $14.7 million at 20 percent and $20.5 million at 21 percent. Hopefully, at some point along the way, you would find ministries in which to profitably invest the interest to stop the stuff from piling up.

Look at the same situation another way. Assume that you put $2,000 away into an untouchable account each year. At the end of forty years you would have $885,000 at a 10 percent return; $3.6 million at 15 percent; $14.7 million at 20 percent and $19.5 million at 21 percent.

Two lessons here: First, the importance of sacrificing early in your career to start accumulating a capital base. The time value of money is incredibly important.

Second, the rate of return is important. The difference of just 1 percent in the above examples (between 20 and 21 percent return) is enormous.

Of course, these examples assume no annual tax on earnings, so the money would have to be invested in a tax-free instrument such as an IRA.

5. Borrowers Become Slaves of Lenders

Look up and down the roads of rural Cedar Falls and you can see a history of farmers enslaved by their lenders. My own experience with a Chicago bank bringing the hammer down is further proof. When borrowing gets to the point where the lender can call in the loan, and in doing so claim control of all your property, you have become a slave to debt.

In a highly volatile world which is underlaid with gradual inflation, we can expect sharp cyclical aberrations which will tend to make leverage look good one year and cash look good the next. Risk-taking is not unbiblical, but it must be done in a prudent manner.

Since there are few solid formulas for prudence, the Christian investor must be humbly led by the Holy Spirit on the amount of debt he assumes.

In your business, you will no doubt run into many speculators. They aren't gamblers. They do play a role in society.

There is a difference between a gambler and a speculator who carefully takes risk. A gambler creates uncertainties for the sport of it. He is reduced to hoping for luck.

The speculator conserves capital for his own profit and for the benefit of future customers. He serves others by entering into market forecasting and taking risks others are unwilling, or can't afford, to bear.

When economic planning is decentralized and decisions are made by owners of private property, society is shielded from the risks of massive centralized error. Thus, a speculator is creating an important function in the preservation of freedom.

On the other hand, a speculator is constantly putting himself at risk and can be wiped out. He should have a money management system in place which never exposes more than 5 percent of his wealth on any risk position.

I know of your interest in speculation, one which you began to learn at my elbow when you were nine years old. I urge caution in taking financial risks.

6. God Wants Us to Live an Abundant Life

Dr. Bill Bright, president of Campus Crusade for Christ, once told an associate that he thought there was no amount of money too large for God to entrust to a man who had no personal desires toward it. As a result, most of the Campus Crusade for Christ ministries are operated in such a way that the directors are responsible for their personal support. They receive no personal gain from successful seminars or fundraising events.

Jabez asked God to bless him. And certainly, God blessed Abraham. It is God's intent that we have plenty, and that we share it with those around us.

If we continually are short of cash, we need to ask ourselves if we have been following the principle of "sowing and reaping." We need to put giving at the top of our priorities: "Seek ye first the kingdom of God . . . and all these things shall be added unto you" (Matthew 6:33, KJV).

The abundant life in the spiritual and physical sense is a result of a life of faith. It is the harvest of sowing good seed (giving).

Money, like any resource, can be wasted if improperly managed. One of the lessons on waste was impressed on my mind in the separator room of the old barn on the "home place."

The separator room was a happy spot. When the evening chores reached this room, it meant the milking was over and it was about time to head for the supper table.

In the separator room the milk was poured through a strainer into a tub, which held the milk until the separator was cranked up to speed. Then we opened a spigot. The milk flowed between spinning discs, which caused the valuable cream to rise to the top. The cream ran out one spout and the lower-valued skimmed milk ran out the other.

How well I remember the lesson of the separator room. While changing pails, I spilled part of a pail. That brought a stern admonition from Dad: "Spilling is wasteful. Skim milk has value. Now don't cry over spilled milk. Just don't spill it again."

Dad was bending my value system so my attitude would reflect the fact that nearly everything has some value. Waste, even of cheap resources, is still waste.

ON THE PATH TOWARD HONOR

1. Honestly evaluate your attitude toward money. Is your desire for wealth all-consuming? What circumstances cause you to hold back on your giving?

2. Are you willing to build a solid financial future by sacrificing now in order to take advantage of the value in compound interest? What cutbacks in spending are you willing to make? Plan to put 10 percent of your earnings into a savings account each month.

3. The principles "God owns it all" and "You can't take it with you" will have a great effect on how you spend your money. Do you spend your money with these principles in mind? In what ways can you "send money ahead" by making a practical investment now in preparation for eternity?

9
GIVING

Activating the Biblical
"Give . . . Get . . . Give More" Cycle

*For if you give, you will get! Your gift will return to
you in full and overflowing measure, pressed down,
shaken together to make room for more, and
running over. Whatever measure you use to give —
large or small — will be used to measure what is
given back to you.*

(Luke 6:38)

Giving out of gratitude to God becomes a cycle
of blessing. You can't outgive Him.

When the Lord talked about giving, He used the
example of the widow's mite to indicate that attitude
is all-important. Even though she hadn't given a large
amount, in God's economy she had given more than
most because she gave all she had.

You are blessed to know your great-grandma Carrie Smith, a giving example to her own and three
succeeding generations. Widowed in her early fifties,
she sold her belongings to move in with my father and
mother when I was about nine years old.

Grandma Carrie cared for the house while Mom

taught school. She was a "second mother" to Larry and me, and had a profound impact on my spiritual life.

In later years, when someone in the family needed help — such as you or your sister Leah — she immediately dropped what she was doing, wiped her hands on her apron and helped the person in need. Her interests were always those of others.

In our most recent visit with Grandma Carrie her health was frail and her problems outnumbered those of most of us. But her first question was, "How are David and Leah?"

To this day your great-grandma is known by friends all over the area as a sweet, giving person. Her reward on earth is a wonderful reputation and a large circle of friends. I can scarcely imagine the rewards which must await her in heaven.

You remember Great-Grandma Carrie as the one who made those outstanding cinnamon rolls and sneaked you an extra one after Mom said you had eaten enough. You remember the stories of her scraping wallpaper off our first home, helping us paint and get settled. She seemed to live to give of herself to others.

That's the attitude we should carry about all of our possessions — one of seeking places to invest those possessions in other people. If we give to others, God gives us more. That's the promise of Luke 6:38 (paraphrased): "If you give, you will get."

But many miss the real blessing in giving because their objective is to get. Giving with the motive of getting reduces this principle to a selfish, mechanical technique aimed at manipulating God.

Giving 77

True Motivation for Giving

The correct motive for giving is to please God. Our desire should be to carry out the loving works He has assigned us as His ambassadors. View this biblical principle as a continuous cycle: Give to receive so you can give more and receive again to give even more...

God has an abundant storehouse, but He doesn't give you more until you give what you already have. Guard against hoarding. Hoarding is the approach Satan uses. He told Eve, "Surely you can have that apple." The three basic attacks of Satan are aimed at getting for yourself: lust of the eyes, lust of the flesh and the pride of life.

So if you give $10 to a poor couple and selfishly pray that God will give you a new Lincoln, you should question your motive. You are missing the whole point and will likely miss the blessing which comes from giving with a servant's heart.

In *Giving Yourself Away*, Larry O'Nan says, "You should always give with the goal of seeking to advance the work of God's kingdom here on earth." He suggests seven steps in applying a biblical approach to giving. He is referring to giving time, talent, possessions and other gifts, as well as money. His suggested process:

1. Give yourself and your possessions to God by relinquishing all your rights.

2. Recognize that God is your total final supply of all you need.

3. Count on Him by faith to empower you with the Holy Spirit. We can't live the life of a steward in our own strength.

4. Begin to give according to His directions.

5. Thank and praise God for the privilege you have of distributing His wealth and resources.

6. Expect results.

7. Give again and again and again.[1]

Paul instructs believers, "Let each one do just as he has purposed in his heart; not grudgingly or under compulsion; for God loves a cheerful giver" (2 Corinthians 9:7, NASB).

The Bible clearly teaches that God owns it all. We give from His abundant supply. We are to give cheerfully. When I have need, I am to ask Him. How I handle what He gives me is important because I reap what I sow.

The Old Testament is filled with examples of God's promised blessing being received in short order. In the New Testament we see both immediate and eternal rewards. It is for this reason we should not be discouraged if we don't see immediate tangible results. Perhaps part, or most, of the reward for some gifts is being credited to our eternal account. In fact, Jesus encourages giving with eternal ends in mind:

> Don't store up treasures here on earth where they can erode away or may be stolen. Store them in heaven where they will never lose their value, and are safe from thieves. If your profits are in heaven your heart will be there, too (Matthew 6:19,20).

ON THE PATH TOWARD HONOR

1. List five different ways you can give of yourself to others. Think of a friend who could use one of those "gifts" on your list and make a plan to give yourself away this week.

2. Examine your motives for giving. Do you find that you give in order to get? Or do you give in order to give more?

10
EFFORT
❧

A Fool-Proof Formula for Results

Work hard and cheerfully at all that you do, just as though you were working for the Lord and not merely for your masters, remembering that it is the Lord Christ who is going to pay you, giving you your full portion of all he owns. He is the one you are really working for.

(Colossians 3:23,24)

Dad had been to a University of Iowa basketball game the night before. As we were finishing the clean-up after milking the cows, he shared the most important part of his trip to Iowa City.

"After the game we went to the locker room. Over the door of the locker room was a statement worth remembering," he told me. He then repeated a saying which was to stay with me as a motivator for life: "A little extra effort makes the difference between mediocrity and greatness."

Your Grandpa Oster was a real example of a person who consistently put forth the extra effort.

Maybe you can improve on his example as you try

it in your own life. Maybe you'll pass the idea along to the young people you advise, and to your children someday.

Energizing Ideas Into Results

Effort × *Time* = *Results*. What that formula really says is that the person putting forth the best effort over the longest time will be the biggest winner.

Of course, the Christian must temper such ideas with the assumption that the effort has God's blessing.

Another way to look at the formula is to add the concept of efficiency.

Effort × *Efficiency* × *Time* = *Results*. Effort alone isn't enough. Dad observed me as a ten-year-old scooping corn out of a bin. I was putting out vigorous effort, with quick and powerful motions. Dad was working a bit slower. Each shovel had the same amount on it. I soon tired and stopped. Dad just kept steadily shoveling on.

It was on the end of that scoop shovel that I got my first lesson in balancing effort with efficiency. "Work steady, or you'll get tired quickly," Dad urged. "Keep your eye and mind on your work so your next move is always in your head. That way you don't have to stop and think what to do next."

Dad's training in the corn bin made it a bit easier for me to accept and apply the time management principles from books I have read over the years.

Recently I summed up my philosophy as I encouraged a new manager to make his time count. I told him to first get his eye on the results he wants to achieve for the year. Then break those results down by quarter and month.

Then I urged him to ask himself what kind of monthly activity would be required to generate those monthly results, and suggested he put those items on a list. From that list of things to do each month, he could pick those which must be done today.

With the results in mind first, he could be sure that the activity of the day was driving him toward the desired end.

Lots of folks focus on time only. They work from morning until night — long, misdirected hours.

Others focus on activity. They are busybodies, with long lists of things to get done. But when they are all done, there has been no accumulation of effort toward a big goal.

Effort has to be balanced with efficiency and time, always keeping a desired goal in mind. You'll find precious few who can see the big picture and are bright enough to sort out the $100-an-hour jobs from the $3-an-hour jobs.

You'll find that the men and women who have this perspective are usually in management, or on their way there. They have the ability to muster many resources toward some specific, desirable end.

There's another element to the formula: talent, or skill. Part of this is God-given, part is learned.

You will find that there are some things which you do with much greater ease and skill than other people. Maybe you have a "knack" for the job, or a spiritual gift. Maybe you have had training and hours of practice which have honed that skill. Either way, the people with the most talent or skill will rise to the top only if they are applying the other elements of the formula.

I have seen more disappointments in this area than in any other. Many promising young men never reach their peak because they burn out quickly (jerky effort), or they don't apply the time ("forty hours a week and no more"), or they never get the big picture and are unproductively busy most of their lives.

So when you add up all the elements, the formula for getting things done looks like this:

Effort × *Efficiency* × *Time* × *Talent* × *God's Will* = *Results*

"Learn an industry cold. Then find a need and fill it," says Ross Perot, an American business success.

ON THE PATH TOWARD HONOR

1. Think back to a situation where the effort made on your part really paid off. (It may be the extra time you spent on a paper you wrote or the long hours you put in training for a big athletic event or the investment of yourself in a relationship.) How did your effort make a difference in the end result?

2. When do you find it difficult to make an effort? List some ways to overcome the barriers that stand between you and desired results.

3. Do you believe the statement "A little extra effort makes the difference between mediocrity and greatness"? Are you willing to make that extra effort in all areas of your life?

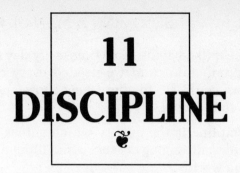

11
DISCIPLINE
❧

The Relationship of Timeliness
to Success

*He went home and knelt down as usual in his
upstairs bedroom, with its windows open toward
Jerusalem, and prayed three times a day, just as he
always had.*

(Daniel 6:10)

Take special note as you step over the door sill
of our old hip-roofed barn which consumed hours of
labor for five generations of Osters. The door sill is a
four-inch wide wooden beam worn almost round by
the footsteps of time. Dad's steps. Granddad's. And all
the kids. These weren't random footsteps. Every 6
A.M. for forty years, men stepped across that sill to
feed and milk the cows.

Regularity bred discipline — one of the characteristics that opens the door to success for all who are
willing to commit. No one ever told us we were learning discipline in those days on the farm. We just knew
there was work to be done; there were cows to be
milked; there were calves to feed. We knew the cows

had to be milked at the same time every day for maximum production. And we needed every ounce of cream we could get to afford new shoes and a new shirt to start school.

Discipline is the quality which shines through again and again among the successful industrial leaders of the world.

The demanding pace of serving on the farm taught early lessons to men who later moved to the top in major corporations. Others learned discipline on a paper route or maybe by working in an office.

You will, no doubt, be given the responsibility of teaching discipline to a new generation. I know you won't forget those cold mornings when, before daybreak, we walked down to that barn to feed your 4-H Club calves. The chill factor dropped to minus-forty on a few of those mornings, yet the calves still had to eat.

You need a "barn" for the next generation's training. Maybe it will be your basement, your garage or the street in front of your house. Somewhere you must find the place and the task where your children can discover the joy of accomplishment which comes with learning to lead a life of discipline.

I believe it's a bit easier for a disciplined person to lead a successful Christian life. Successful Christian living is being a disciple of Jesus Christ. He says, "Follow me and I will make you fishers of men." That's a daily opportunity which leads to a life of significance to those willing to pay the price.

The Early Bird Gets the Worm

Let's walk across the barn to the east door for a

lesson closely related to discipline.

What a view! You can look through the orchard
and see the east eighty acres, and on across the valley
to three neighboring farms. That barn door provides a
view to the outside world. That view, when accom-
panied by a little of Dad's coaching, became another
classroom.

At the end of a hard day's work it was good to
pause and lean on the door and let your eyes rest on
the view of the valley, the creek and the gently rolling
hills. Little did I realize, at the time, the lessons of life
creeping out of those hills.

More than once I recall looking over one of the
neighbor's pastures in the morning and hearing my
father say, "It's 7 o'clock and those cows are still in the
field. At 9, those folks will still be in the barn milking
their cows. But we'll be on the tractor, getting a full
day of fieldwork done. Son, the early bird gets the
worm."

Timeliness. Twelve years later a Purdue University computer verified to me the high value of timeliness. It said farmers who get crops planted on time
earn $50 to $100 more per acre than farmers who are
late. Time at crucial moments was worth hundreds of
dollars an hour. Dad had no computer. He just observed through the barn door — a window to the
practical lessons of the world — that neighbors who
didn't get their milking done on time got their crops
planted late. That meant they cultivated late and har-
vested late.

Working hard is important. But getting the right
job done at the right time is more important. There's a
whole chapter on timeliness in Peter Drucker's man-

agement book, read by thousands of big-shot executives the world over. We didn't know about the book when we were working on the farm, but right through this barn door I learned the principle of timeliness with my own eyes at age fifteen. You will find similar object lessons in the real world to teach your children.

Take a deep breath of that fresh air while you're standing here. You know, this door is big enough for two men to stand shoulder to shoulder, sometimes chatting in relaxed tones, sometimes just looking and thinking independently, but always standing together waiting for the right moment to move the milkers to the next pair of cows.

ON THE PATH TOWARD HONOR

1. How do you practice the art of discipline in your life? Think of a situation when your commitment to discipline brought about positive results. How would that outcome have been different had you not kept your commitment to discipline?

2. How important is getting the right things done at the right time in your life? Think of an opportunity you missed because what needed to be done wasn't completed on time. What kept you from meeting your deadline? How can you avoid those barriers next time?

12
WITNESSING
❦

Sharing the Answer to Life's Problems

Therefore go and make disciples in all nations, baptizing them in the name of the Father and of the Son and of the Holy Spirit.

(Matthew 28:19)

There are really three very important functions of a Christian. First, as disciples, we are to become Christ-like. Second, we are to make disciples by telling others of the benefits of walking with Christ and instructing them how to become Christians. Third, we must disciple young believers to encourage their spiritual growth.

The heart of this book is on becoming Christ-like: finding true success in life by becoming more like Him in attitude, conversation and action. A very important aspect of your Christian walk is telling others about Christ, or witnessing.

Although the word *witnessing* is frequently associated with the door-to-door, "cold calling" approach, there is a much more effective way to use your current position in life to win souls. "Lifestyle evangelism" seeks to be alert for opportunities to share the gospel with those you have "earned a right" to have as an audience. Neighbors, friends, relatives and work associates are people God puts in your pathway.

A casual conversation in the back yard with a neighbor might surface a problem in his personal life. Your response might go something like this: "John, I'll put that matter on my prayer list. Is that something you do, too? Tap the power of God through prayer?" Your response can lead to an opportunity to explain the gospel.

Your consistency on the job, or your mild, unflappable manner in a crisis might prompt a peer to ask, "What's different about you, Dave? You appear to be so confident, and peaceful."

A question like that is a priceless moment that months, or years, have earned you. It is a signal that you have "earned a right" to be heard. How you respond to questions like that could make the difference in whether or not that person will hear the gospel. Use the time, either at that moment or by setting up an appointment later in the day, to have a conversation about the Lord.

Such a conversation could include a presentation of The Four Spiritual Laws pamphlet by Campus Crusade for Christ, or some similar clear presentation of the gospel. As a good salesman must ask for the "close," a disciple must invite the unsaved into the kingdom. That's our number one purpose in life: to tell others about Christ and invite them to follow Him.

Don't worry about what your friends or business

associates might say. Don't worry about whether they
actually receive Christ at the moment of your invitation. Our job as Christians is to present the gospel
message and leave the rest to the Holy Spirit.

Divine Appointments

I was tending to matters of business at the office
one morning when a co-worker of four years dropped
a memo on my desk, greeted me and then blurted,
"There's something really different about you. How
do you remain so positive?" That question opened an
hour-long conversation. Although I had opened staff
conferences with prayer and frequently used staff
meetings as an opportunity to present the claims of
Christ, I had had no previous spiritual person-to-
person conversation with this man.

We talked about the only reason I could really be
optimistic — my assurance that even if I die, I know
I'll be victorious and will spend eternity in heaven.
We talked about Jesus Christ, His claim to be God and
His statement that He is the only way to a right rela-
tionship with God.

Then, I simply asked if he would like this same
relationship by repenting of his sins and asking Jesus
to come into his life as Lord and Savior. He did. He left
the office a Christian.

On another occasion a fellow stopped in looking
for help to find a job. He was flat broke. His string of
"tough luck" stories was twenty minutes long. After
listening to his problems, I said, "Wow! You have too
many problems to handle all by yourself. What you
really need is a personal relationship with Jesus
Christ, so He can direct you through." His response: "I
sure do."

Right there in my office he acknowledged his sinfulness and his need. Then in a broken, non-theological prayer, he invited Jesus Christ into his life.

These were special situations set up by divine appointment. I share them with you only as an example of what to look for. When you see the "open door," be prepared to help your friends or business associates by giving them a drink from the "well that never runs dry."

You don't have to be a preacher to use these opportunities...just a friend interested in helping another find lasting answers to the problems in life. We have the answer to trouble, problems, worry, despair, estrangement, feelings of insecurity or insignificance — a personal relationship with the Lord we know.

Tell others whenever you get a chance. I'll *guarantee* you that if you ask the Lord, He will put some opportunities in your path. Use them wisely. You may be the *only* person the Lord chooses to use to reach certain people in your circle of influence.

ON THE PATH TOWARD HONOR

1. In what ways can you "earn the right" to be heard by your friends and acquaintances? How do you develop relationships that can lead to witnessing opportunities?

2. What keeps you from witnessing? Take time this week to share these fears with a mature Christian friend who is an active witness.

3. Are you prepared for the "divine appointments" God has waiting for you? Have you gone to
Him in prayer, asking for wisdom when those opportunities arise? Plan a response you could make when
you're asked what's different about you.

13
INNER LIFE
❧

Exercising Spiritual Principles for Personal Growth

That is why we never give up. Though our bodies are dying, our inner strength in the Lord is growing every day.

(2 Corinthians 4:16)

"**L**et's pray," says the first person headed for bed. "Time to pray," calls the second voice down the hall. "We're going to pray," echoes another. "Where's Leah?" questions one of us.

Such was the final activity around home nearly every night. Those sounds bouncing down the hallway drew us to the foot of a bed, usually in the master bedroom.

Great moments. Everything stopped as we praised God, invited the Lord to direct us, invoked His help in many areas, interceded for many others, sought the Holy Spirit's bidding in our lives.

No big deal. We just did it. Regularly. Regardless

of how motivated we were at the moment. It was amazing how personal conflicts melted away as we presented ourselves together before God.

This is spiritual discipline. This is exercising spiritual fundamentals with the attitude of an athlete training for a big event.

Spiritual discipline is practiced with an end in view: to sharpen spiritual sensitivity. To hear God speak.

That's why spiritual discipline usually involves a quiet spot. There's a quiet spot in the home where one can find uninterrupted time to read, pray, meditate, praise, worship. There's another quiet spot that needs to be developed — it's that quiet spot we can return to in our own heart. We gather our strength in those quiet times before the Lord.

We feed that quiet spot in our communion with the Lord. There are no quick, cheap substitutes for this time of feeding, or "spiritual inhaling" as Bill Bright of Campus Crusade for Christ calls it. This is absorbing what God has to say to you.

In a second-story room in Ames, Iowa, I was alone for one six-week summer session. Friends had gone home. I stayed to work at the radio station.

At night I returned with a light load of homework. But I also read and studied the Epistles. There, alone, I came to know Christ in a deep and personal way.

I got beyond spiritual cliches to something very personal. When I got on my knees to pray, it was as if the Lord were sitting on the bed listening.

These experiences of deepening our relationship with the Lord, of yielding more territory in our life totally to His control, are usually the result of quietness of the spirit. Sometimes those experiences are brought on by crisis, sometimes by a serious and prayerful resolve to know God, and sometimes by the regular discipline of submitting to God in every area.

Reading Scripture, praying, worshiping, meditating, serving others — these are all spiritual disciplines.

But how do you get this process started when you have been through a period of spiritual dryness? In my life, other Christians' excitement for the Lord has rubbed off on me. Reading books by authors who could pull together topics and make them come alive from Scripture has often led me deeper into the Bible itself. Sometimes I have been driven to Scripture in response to needing a right answer for a committee, in making a speech, or in sharing the gospel with someone.

Perhaps the greatest motivator for spiritual discipline is viewing the world from God's perspective and realizing that men and women all around us are living their lives and heading for eternity without God. A knowledge of Scripture helps us help them.

Robert Foster's *Celebration of Discipline* and Gordon MacDonald's *Ordering Your Private World* are two works which have helped me most in recent years in the area of personal spiritual discipline.

If there is order in your inner life, there will be a sense of peace and direction about you which will speak to others. One day someone will ask, "What's different about you?" That's your on-the-job opportunity to explain the work of Jesus Christ in your own life.

Since our main objective in life is to prepare others for the kingdom, such "divine appointments" with fellow men are the *real* opportunities of a lifetime.

I'm confident that many such appointments lie ahead for you. Order your inner life through disciplined reading of Scripture, prayer, worship, praise, meditation and service in preparation for these great moments.

Master these disciplines in the easy times. Then, in the big and little crises that come up in life, you will have reserve strength to pull you through.

Your power of good judgment, your freedom from fear, your confidence in direction all find their foundation in regular exercise of the spiritual disciplines.

ON THE PATH TOWARD HONOR

1. Where is your "quiet spot"? What can you do to keep your time with the Lord from becoming dull and routine?

2. Pick one area of spiritual discipline (Scripture reading and memorization, prayer, worship, meditation, etc.) and make it your special focus during your time with the Lord for the next three months. Set a goal to read at least one book on the subject. Study Scripture passages that address the discipline. What benefits can you see in your life from the practice of spiritual discipline?

14
RELATIONSHIPS
❦

The Importance of the Company You Keep

Don't think only of yourself. Try to think of the other fellow, too, and what is best for him.
                                             (1 Corinthians 10:24)

A new commandment I give to you, that you love one another, even as I have loved you, that you will also love one another. By this all men will know that you are My disciples, if you have love for one another.   *(John 13:34,35)*

Your mom and I were chatting with some folks on the front steps of the tiny Lake Geneva, Wisconsin, Bible Chapel when they cordially invited us over for dinner. That invitation changed our lives.

Although your mom and I had been Christians since childhood, Ray and Laura Routley showed us how a committed Christian family lives. They became our friends. Their home was always open. Laura held the first baby shower for your mom when she was carrying you. They regularly led us to Scripture for answers to our questions, causing us to want to know more about God's Word. Their friendship led us to other friendships with people we still see from time to time. To this day, Ray and Laura regularly pray for us, and we for them. I hope you find such friendships early in your adult life.

You are known by the company you keep. Your choices in the next few months are absolutely critical.

Obviously, the quality of your relationship with the Lord is of utmost importance. Unfortunately, some folks look to the Lord for salvation, then they rule their own lives. They deny Him the open relationship which He wants with them. He wants to speak to us through His Word and the Holy Spirit. He wants us to claim promises in prayer.

The world needs more men who are committed to seek the mind of God, to know more about the Lord, to deepen their faith in Him. Your relationship with God will determine the direction of all your other relationships.

You will be attracted to, and will attract, three kinds of friends: those who are chasing purely worldly objectives, those who want a cloak of Christianity to cover their selfish ways, and those who are truly committed Christians. You will, no doubt, have friends in all three categories. But ultimately you will feel most comfortable with one of the groups, hopefully the last.

A man committed to the cause of Christ will tend to attract committed Christians and those truly seeking answers to big issues. You have this God-given ability to attract people to important causes. There is no greater cause than advancing the kingdom.

As a two-year-old, when the boundaries of your world were outlined by a backyard fence, your mom and I observed something about you which has stuck with you for life. You made friends easily.

You used to hang on the fence bordering Mr. Reilly's driveway and make conversation with him. He called you a "character" because you had a sense of humor that attracted this adult neighbor.

Since neighborhood boys were in short supply, you made up a friend. You talked to him. When asked, you would say you were playing with "Charlie Brown." You would frequently warn your mom and me to be careful where we walked so we wouldn't step on "my friend Charlie."

If I was moving around the house and not giving you attention as a toddler, you'd say "dub-a-dee" and slap the top step between the kitchen and living room. That was my signal to sit beside you and talk. You would ask me questions. I'd ask you questions. For some reason, I chose to talk straight to you with none of the typical "baby talk."

We talked about rocks and trees and fences and streets and flowers and all the do's and don'ts relating to those things. In spite of our talks you occasionally threw the rocks, climbed the trees and fences, got into the street, and stepped on the flowers.

When Grandpa came on weekends, he'd follow your instruction to "dub-a-dee." He'd check out all the do's and don'ts in your life. "What does Daddy do if you climb the fence?" he inquired once. You replied straight-faced, "Daddy spank Day-dee." Your quick sense of humor and ability to relate with people has won the hearts of folks far beyond your family.

Rich relationships with people are one of life's true treasures. Develop these relationships with lots of friends, then yield them to the Lord. He will allow you to be a blessing to your friends in a very special way.

ON THE PATH TOWARD HONOR

1. Describe your relationship with the Lord. In what ways does this relationship affect all your other relationships?

2. Who are your friends? What do these friendships say about you? Are people attracted to you for the right reasons?

15
SACRIFICE

One Thanksgiving Example

And you husbands, show the same kind of love to your wives as Christ showed to the church when he died for her.

(Ephesians 5:25)

The world of men has two extreme types, neither of which is biblical. There's the wimp who can't make a decision on his own. He looks around first to see where everybody else is, then jumps onto the most popular bandwagon.

At the other end of the scale is the bulldozer-type, who believes he is the authority in every situation and who has no feelings for those around him.

In the home, the wimp and the bulldozer are equal threats. The wimp constantly defers to his wife and family. In the absence of a man who can make decisions and lead, the woman becomes the leader and decision-maker. She is the initiator. She directs the affairs of the family. God didn't plan it that way.

On the other hand, the dominant male who considers no one else in his decision-making process creates feelings of inferiority in his wife and children. His bossy, self-centered style creates antagonism, which sets the stage for bitter confrontation. This leads to development of emotional scars which sometimes stay with the children of a bulldozer-led home for the remainder of their lives.

A home out of godly order is frequently in emotional chaos. The improper role models for the children sow seeds of future problems that can be passed down the family tree for generations.

The model man, in the context of marriage, is explained in Ephesians 5:25: "And you husbands, show the same kind of love to your wives as Christ showed to the church when he died for her."

The Way to Headship

What does that really mean today? First, Christ was the initiator. He offered Himself as sacrifice for sin. We are responders to His offer of freedom from the penalty and power of sin.

Christ loved us sacrificially — to the point of giving His life for the church. By His death, He defined love as action on behalf of another.

If sacrifice is your heart attitude, you won't be tempted to use the phony excuses for self-centered living which many couples use when they break up a marriage.

"We are growing apart" is only an indication that total sacrifice may be a bigger price than either wants to pay. The excuse that "the romance has gone out of our marriage" is an admission that emotional experience, not a meaningful biblical relationship, is the goal.

Your relationship with the woman who will become your wife should be based on your caring for her so much that you will make great personal sacrifices to further her interests.

David, I must admit to you that this is a lesson I am only beginning to learn in my own life. I wish I could hold myself up as a good example and say, "Follow me." I can't, yet.

Instead, use your mother as an example. After twenty-five years of marriage, I am now beginning to realize that her sacrifices on behalf of the rest of us have frequently gone unappreciated. We have the rest of our lives to correct that, however.

It is so easy for us to be the recipients of high levels of performance from a wife and mother and just assume this is the minimum acceptable standard, making anything less a basis for complaint.

Just consider Thanksgiving dinner as one example of your mom's sacrifice. It's a wonderful day, and it stays in our memories as a great time of fellowship around family members, food and football.

I like to sleep in, take a morning run with some runner friends in town, shower, catch the Thanksgiving Day parades on TV as the family gathers, chat, feast on a tremendous meal, retire to the family room for lazy conversation while we watch the Lions and the Redskins, grab a few popcorn balls during the afternoon, feast on cookies and candies later in the day and say "Isn't Thanksgiving great?" when it is all over.

Your mom, on the other hand, gets up about 5:30 on Thanksgiving morning. She quietly moves down the hall so she won't disturb the sleeping family and heads for the turkey. She stuffs it, pours on the juices and puts it in the oven. She may get back to bed by 6:30 for a few brief moments before I begin rattling around, trying to find my running clothes.

She hears me rustling around looking for something, and sits up to point out that I am standing on the shorts I am looking for. There they are, folded next to my running socks, just where she put them the night before.

I jump into my clean sweat clothes, also neatly hung the night before. They are in the same place in the laundry room closet so they will be easy for me to find. (She got to bed late the night before because she was finishing the washing, including the sacks full of clothes brought back by her two college-student children.)

About the time I get ready to go out the door, Mom comes to the kitchen to kiss me good-bye. I apologize for waking her up while finding my running shorts. She says that's OK, she was awake anyway.

With one foot out the door I offer, "Is there anything I can do for you, sweetheart?" "No, things are pretty well under control," she reassures me. I know there is lots of work to do. She knows I know there's lots of work to do, but she lets me head off to town to make the seven-mile run with my friends with a clear conscience.

I get back by 10 A.M. You and Leah are sleepy-eyed in the family room sharing tales of the late hours you have kept the week before as you crammed for tests. Feeling sorry, Mom offers you hot chocolate served in the family room so you won't have to move your tired bones.

In the meantime, she has cleaned and cut carrots, celery and other greens that can be "gotten out of the way early." She has the rolls lined up, ready to be popped into the oven. The corn she froze last summer is being thawed, and the table is set. While I was running she transformed the house into a facility fit for entertaining.

"Pick up your feet," she requests as she runs the vacuum cleaner one more time through the house. Rather than offering to help, we might mutter something like, "You don't have to clean the house again. It looks great just like it is."

My conscience finally pricked, I rise to the occasion and issue a few orders: "David, get your room in order. Leah, finish setting the table." I dash down to bring up the extra chairs needed to seat the family.

"Anything else I can do?" we usually ask as we are returning to our easy chairs to watch the parade. "No, things are pretty well in order," Mom reassures us as she scurries from one room to another finishing her mental list of "to do's" before company arrives.

The company arrives. Mom asks me to bring the turkey up from the oven downstairs. In the midst of all the company coming in and out of the kitchen, I put on the apron and begin carving the turkey. (This activity makes it appear as though I am an integral part in the success of the whole affair.) Leah usually helps me so I don't make a complete mess of it, however.

Mom is doing something every moment. I'm never sure exactly what, but it always adds up to everything getting done right on time for all the pieces to fit on the table at exactly the same moment. How she manages the timing, only she can tell.

There we sit, as I give thanks for this beautiful spread which God has provided. And it is beautiful. Sweet potatoes, turkey, cranberry sauce, sweet corn, a special "holidays-only" frozen salad, hot rolls, relishes and all the trimmings topped off with pumpkin pie and ice cream.

Of course, we thank Mom for the fantastic meal. Maybe we even pick a few things off the table and return the empty bowls to the kitchen to ease our consciences, but our minds are on a comfortable seat for the football game.

Six touchdowns, three fumbles and two pass interceptions later, Mom reappears in the family room with cold drinks, cookies, popcorn balls and candy for all. What fun! Finally, three hours after dinner, with the Lions well ahead and the game beginning to get boring, Mom reappears with empty hands, ready to enjoy visiting with relatives.

That's about the time Grandma Carrie thinks she should begin getting back home. And one by one, over the next hour, the house empties.

Mom had some good conversation with the family, but it was while she was moving from place to place serving them.

Now, with the dishes all cleaned, the fine silver put back in the drawer and the house returned to normal we say something like, "Isn't it just great to have the family filling the house on Thanksgiving?" "Just great," is Mom's tired reply.

I have no idea of the hours of preparation that go into making popcorn balls, three-bean salad and all the nice little things which make a day like that complete. But I do know that Thanksgiving Day is only a slightly different example of the everyday sacrifice in the life of your mother for us.

Christ wants us to love our wives like He loves us — sacrificially. In His absence, He has sent a few modern-day role models. You and I have lived with one — your mom!

The Bible encourages us to "esteem others greater than ourselves." You are fortunate to have witnessed an example of that attitude lived out in your mom. May each of us learn from the Lord's example of sacrifice, as well as that of people like your mom. We will be better men if we learn servant leadership and apply the principle in our homes, churches and businesses.

Oster men have some bulldozer tendencies, and a streak of self-sufficiency. We would do well to practice more loving, sacrificial service to each other and to those around us. In doing so, we acknowledge our dependence upon others in the body of Christ for a sense of true fulfillment.

Scripture tells us, "He who shall be first (the leader), shall be last (the sacrificial servant)."

I'll start by resolving to be a better helper on Thanksgiving Day.

ON THE PATH TOWARD HONOR

1. Which extreme type do you tend toward — the wimp or the bulldozer? What are the dangers inherent

in both types of personalities?

2. Is sacrifice your "heart attitude"? List some practical ways you can show a servant spirit to those around you at home, work, school and church. Take four of those ideas and during the next month implement one a week.

3. Think of someone in your life who has been an example of servant leadership. What have they taught you about leadership? What qualities do they possess that you see a need for in your life?

16
LIFE PARTNERS
❦

Eight Marks of Maturity
To Look For

*The man who finds a wife finds a good thing; she is
a blessing to him from the Lord.*

(Proverbs 18:22)

As I pen these words, the waves of the Atlantic
Ocean are gently rolling in on the shores of Delray
Beach, Florida. You know that I have always worked
hard, but subscribe to the philosophy that "all work
and no play makes Jack a dull boy."

Your mom and I are enjoying a business/vacation
trip which we have made to this part of the country
every year for more than ten years. Last night we had a
quiet dinner for two at a window table overlooking
the Boca Inlet. In this, our twenty-fifth year of marriage, I plan to take your mom to some special place
each month for an "anniversary year" celebration.
The traditional picture in the paper and open house
just don't interest us.

At these special evenings alone, we have been recounting some of the great times of the past, and we've been doing some thinking about the future. We're having a great time together.

You have seen us at our best and our worst. You recall a few stormy days in those twenty-five years and have probably learned by our bad example a few lessons on what not to do in your marriage. But we have worked through problems. We are two very different people with completely different strengths and weaknesses. God works these differences into the complete whole that gives marriage a unique strength.

In fact, that's the relationship God established at creation. He first created man. Then he created woman, uniquely different, although equal, as a completer. It is our hope that your mate will play that key role in your life.

It's good to prepare yourself for marriage with an accurate assessment of yourself and the woman you are considering. Unfortunately, most marriage counseling doesn't take place until the date is set and wedding plans are in place. I strongly urge you to attend a weekend seminar, such as the seminars Dennis and Barbara Rainey conduct for Campus Crusade for Christ's Family Ministry, well before your wedding day.

Your mom and I joined hundreds of folks at such a meeting a few months ago and have encouraged others to attend because it provides the basis for understanding each other's needs. The seminar lays a biblical basis for our expectations of each other and spells out clearly our responsibility before God for our mate.

Building Your Mate's Self-Esteem, by the Raineys

and *Becoming One,* by Don Meredith, contain many of the principles of this seminar and should be at the top of your reading list as you approach engagement and marriage.

The Raineys point out in their book that our society's relentless drive for self-fulfillment is sowing the seeds of disaster in marriages. Say the Raineys:

> We are a restless, self-indulgent society whose members often use each other to gain the acceptance they feel they deserve. Thus, we feel used and not genuinely needed, valued or appreciated ... Society applauds people for what they have *done* and what they have *acquired* with seldom an ovation for who they *are.* Our culture says self-esteem is to be built on self-achievement. We feel we must be production-minded, so we generally don't cultivate the relationships that would foster feelings of lasting significance. As a result, we are being "driven" in the wrong direction by a wrong standard of value.[1]

In a marriage with one or both partners insecure in their self-esteem and afraid to reach out, there is a tendency to wait for the *other* to act first, to get the *other* to meet the needs.

"Unfortunately, when a mate's weaknesses surface in the marriage, couples turn on each other," say the Raineys. That's why it's a good idea to accurately assess each other's self-esteem before the weaknesses surface in the marriage.

The "Self-Esteem Inventory" at the end of this chapter is from the Raineys' book and is a suggested starting point on this critical issue.

Finding and Being the Right Mate

You need to strike a balance between logically reasoning through a possible marriage situation, and accepting what God tells you in the quietness of your prayer and meditation with Him.

If your daily prayer is, "Lord, lead me to the woman of Your choice for life," and if your life is in obedience to Him and your daily sins are confessed to Him, you have His promise that He will hear and answer your prayer. Unconfessed sin or unresolved conflict with other believers can hinder your prayer and cloud the clear message God wants to send you.

Chances are, when your "Miss Right" comes along, you will sense an inner peace, and you will receive some confirming words of encouragement from godly men who have known you for some time.

Again I suggest you read Marilyn Heavilin's *Mother to Daughter*. It will give you some valuable insight into how women think and feel, and you will be able to recognize your own "Miss Right" more quickly.

The time you spend in meditation and prayer is absolutely critical at this juncture of your life. No day passes without your mom and I joining with you in prayer on the issue of your Christian growth and the selection of a mate who will be your "completion."

May I suggest to you one of the most important Bible studies I have ever conducted? It is a study of the beatitudes in Matthew 5:1-16. A few years ago I made this my theme passage for the year, reading it over and over repeatedly, probing the minds of other authors who had written on the portion, preaching several messages from it — all in the hope that the saturation of this portion of Scripture would cultivate an atmosphere in which God could mold and shape me.

Many months later I found Don Meredith's book, *Becoming One*, and his eight-point outline. These are

marks of spiritual maturity you should look for in a
mate. These marks should be evident in your own life
also to be a good mate.

1. *Poor in spirit.* The person who is poor in spirit
acknowledges he or she has no real internal power; it
all comes from eternal God. With that attitude in
marriage it is easy to accept someone else's weakness,
because you profess no strength of your own. True
humility stems from one's poverty of spirit. This
doesn't imply weakness or spinelessness. Just the
opposite is the case.

2. *Mournful.* In this portion of Scripture the
mourning is in relation to sin. A mournful person
hates sin and hates to hurt anyone. When he does hurt
someone, his sorrow is real. A marriage partner who
is mournful in this sense can't hold a grudge.

3. *Gentle.* Jesus, by his example, pursued what
was right, but handled correction gently. Remember
how he told the prostitute to "go and sin no more"? "A
gentle person doesn't pout or get depressed when
stress is encountered," says Meredith on this point. "A
gentle person has a quiet confidence which is based
on a knowledge of God's power to solve whatever
problem may be in the path."

4. *Hunger for righteousness.* Seek a mate and be a
mate whose desire, above all else, is to do God's will,
to know God better. If your ambitions in this area
aren't consistent, the two of you will tend to live at the
spiritual level of the one with the weakest interests.

5. *Merciful.* Outgoing kindness is a characteristic
that drives people to do good deeds for others with no
expectation of anything in return. You might call it
compassion. Do you and the mate you choose respond

to the failure and unfortunate situations of others? If you determine to spend some time or money helping someone else, will your mate share your concern, or will she be jealous about the time with you she has lost or the money that was used?

6. *Pure in heart.* Look for signs of honesty and pure motives in your future mate. Be wary of manipulative acts intended to achieve selfish ends. The person who is pure in heart truly sees God. This mate is loyal and is transparent about personal failures.

7. *Peacemaker.* If you are at peace with God, you can be at peace with yourself and, therefore, can be a peacemaker with others. Peacemakers solve problems with truth and love. Is there a tendency to sow discord or peace in the pattern of your life and that of your girlfriend?

8. *Persecuted.* When you put the opinion of God above the opinion of others, there will be criticism. Are you and your mate willing to really stand for what is right to the point of being criticized?[2]

A mate who has these characteristics will be the salt and the light of the world, as well as an excellent marriage partner.

Meredith suggests that if you have serious reservations about how you or your future mate stack up on any of these issues, you should wait before you marry.

"In everything you do, put God first, and he will direct you and crown your efforts with success" (Proverbs 3:6).

ON THE PATH TOWARD HONOR

1. What do you desire in a mate? What do you

desire for your marriage? Have you spent time in prayer and meditation asking for God's guidance in leading you to your life partner?

2. What spiritual qualities have you developed that will enable you to be a good mate? What qualities are you looking for in the woman you want to be your mate?

SELF-ESTEEM INVENTORY[3]

A. Read through this list of descriptions. Using the following scale, rate yourself, then ask your mate to rate himself for each description:

U = Usually   S = Sometimes   R = Rarely

Self	DESCRIPTION	Mate
_____	Fears change	_____
_____	Is introspective	_____
_____	Fears rejection	_____
_____	Seeks to identify with accomplishments	_____
_____	Is critical of self	_____
_____	Is easily discouraged	_____
_____	Is preoccupied with past	_____
_____	Is defensive	_____
_____	Is driven by performance	_____
_____	Talks negatively of self	_____
_____	Seeks identity through position	_____
_____	Lacks decisiveness	_____
_____	Is critical of others	_____
_____	Tends to question self	_____
_____	Compares self to others	_____
_____	Fears failure	_____
_____	Tends to believe the worst about a situation	_____
_____	Can be paralyzed by own inadequacies	_____
_____	Seeks identity through accumulation of wealth	_____
_____	Has difficulty establishing meaningful relationships	_____
_____	Hides weakness	_____
_____	Attempts to control others to make self look good	_____
_____	Is generally satisfied with self	_____
_____	Seeks identity through association with significant others	_____
_____	Is self-conscious	_____
_____	Has negative feelings about self	_____
_____	Has unreal expectations of self	_____
_____	Worries about what others think	_____
_____	Needs continual approval	_____
_____	Is insecure around others	_____
_____	Has difficulty opening up	_____
_____	Takes things personally	_____

B. Compare and discuss your list with your mate's list.

C. Which one or two areas tend to be major struggling points for your mate? For you?

D. Write down what your mate recommends that you do to help him in his major problem area(s).

17
MARRIAGE
🍎

Being a Wise Leader

You wives, submit yourselves to your husbands, for that is what the Lord has planned for you. And you husbands must be loving and kind to your wives and not bitter against them, nor harsh.

(Colossians 3:18,19)

One of the trends in modern society is an up-side-down relationship between men and women. Men are abdicating their proper role as head of the family. Women, sometimes out of necessity, have stepped into a lead role. The lack of role models creates a situation where each generation slips further and further from the ideal.

Recently I took your mom and sister to a movie. Sitting in front of us were two young women, probably in their early twenties. Before the movie began, one of them talked loudly and aggressively with the young men in the row ahead of her. She got up and dashed three rows down the aisle and engaged a second group in conversation. She put her hands on one fellow's shoulder and neck and flirted. Then she changed seats again and threw her legs over the chair in front of her in full view of both groups of men.

This brassy, aggressive, flirting woman was initiating all the action, a trend all too common among young women, I'm afraid — even sometimes among Christian women whose training should have taught them better.

On the male side, I frequently see wimpy men, sitting on their hands waiting to be pursued by a woman — to be overwhelmed by her approach. Aggressive women who initiate action with men and wimpy men who are too timid to initiate anything are symptoms of a society that is abandoning its biblical moorings.

That's not the order God had in mind. Elisabeth Elliot writes to her nephew in *The Mark of a Man*, "Eve was made to order. God saw the shape of Adam's need and designed the woman to fit it exactly in every way. She was the adapter. When you're looking for the right woman to marry, Pete, look for one who is prepared to adapt to you. If you find a woman who is ready to go where you go and do what you do without brooding about being her own person, you'll have found a treasure."[1]

Your mom is such a woman. She was willing to cut short her career in X-ray technology to become a full-time homemaker and responder to my needs and yours. When my travels kept me away from home for a night or two during the week, she kept things going. You had a helper on your paper route. I had a helper on the many loose ends I left behind. When I needed encouragement, your mom always seemed to know it hours before I did. On the big decisions we have faced in life she always had input, but in the final analysis her attitude has been, "You lead, I'll follow."

I thank God she does not believe in the modern concept of a 50/50 marriage where each partner demands that the other carry his or her equal weight. In some areas, like caring for the home, your mom carried 100 percent of the load at times. In other areas, such as making our family financially solvent, I have taken the bulk of the responsibility. The ideal marriage is not 50/50 but 100/100 — each partner giving 100 percent toward the benefit of the other. Though we haven't always been successful, your mom and I have worked toward maintaining that ideal through the years.

Leadership With Love

To attract and satisfy a godly woman, you must be the loving head of your family. You must take charge. That doesn't mean becoming a tyrant. It means carrying out your responsibilities in a tender way.

You are to be "the head of the woman even as Christ is the head of the church." That's with love.

You must lead. <u>As much as you can</u>, be the "idea person" who thinks up interesting places to go, things to do, people to meet and places to serve. Then listen for her response. <u>Be sensitive.</u>

On the other hand, remember that the husband who is a wise leader does not dictate only his ideas. Instead, he provides an open environment for creative sharing of ideas. He is not threatened by his wife's abilities or intimidated by her intelligence. He welcomes and seriously considers her insight and wisdom when they must face major decisions. He is not afraid to encourage her to express her own ideas, and he gives her the freedom to carry them out and to develop her own personality.

<u>Leading is the manly thing to do</u>. You will give your girlfriend, and later your wife, an opportunity to be a responder if you act first as the leader. This gives her a *reason* to respond.

Prayer leadership and encouragement of family members toward their individual spiritual growth should come from the head of the family. Obviously, many godly women have had to fill the gap left by men who neglect their duty, but that's not God's order. <u>You lead in Bible reading and prayer.</u>

You don't have to be a preacher or a spiritual giant to fulfill this obligation. You are responsible to establish and maintain a regular family Bible study time and to see that a sense of its importance is communicated to your family. As the spiritual leader, you are to shepherd the spiritual nourishment and growth of those in your care.

As your family reaches maturity, nothing will compare with the warm memories they'll have of the times Dad opened the Bible and read to his family.

There's a place for praying out loud just with your wife, too. Mom and I sometimes hold hands and pray as we kneel by the bedside. I pray. She prays. We have placed our individual burdens before the Lord. In the process they become shared burdens just by verbalizing them in God's presence.

I attended a men's prayer meeting while in Scottsdale, Arizona, on business recently. The speaker, a seventy-year-old man, testified to the power of prayer when he and his wife joined hands and took their burdens before the Lord.

This Christian man had once been a member of Al Capone's gang and a one-time killer of anyone who got in his way. When he met the Savior he left the gang. Made tender by his relationship with the Lord, and by his years, he related, "Our daughter was running with the wrong crowd and drifting deeper and deeper into the world. So Mother and I prayed out loud as we held hands by the bed. Within weeks, when school started, new friendships were formed. Our daughter turned around."

This dear old man of experience held a crowd of a hundred or more Scottsdale businessmen spellbound as he said, "Gentlemen, I have only a grade school education, so I can't explain family prayer in fancy theological terms. All I can say is that it works."

Lead by noticing little things about your girlfriend, and later, your wife. The success of most relationships doesn't rest on only a few big areas of agreement, but also on a continual flow of exchange of small things — courtesies such as opening a door, a brief unexpected phone call, a note, a wink, a flower, an "I love you."

At the dating stage, lead by taking note of the responses you get. Some people are grateful for the little things you do for them. Others have specific and demanding expectations based on their "rights." Watch out for the woman who demonstrates the latter. People don't change their basic character the moment they say "I do." In fact, Proverbs 27:15,16 indicates that changing the habits of a nagging, contentious woman is about as easy as stopping the wind or grasping oil with your hand.

Your role as the head of the family is to love and

lead — and accept the responsibility. The wise leader will keep Ephesians 5:21 in mind, where we are admonished to "honor Christ by submitting to each other." There will be times when your wife will have a better understanding of a situation or when she may feel it necessary to point out in love that you might be straying from God's best path. God has designed women with a marvelous capacity for blending the mental and emotional options in a far more sensitive way than we men usually think of. You need to welcome and encourage your future wife's expression of those concepts. Loving leadership will maintain a balance of mutual submission.

If you carry out your role in the same spirit of self-sacrifice and service to others which the Lord displayed as the head of His church, you're on the road to a happy marital and family relationship.

Remember, for the most part you're to be the activator, she should be the responder. At the dating stage, if she is continually leading or if you don't like the responses you get from her, don't be afraid to ask her what errors you may be making as an initiator/ leader.

In marriage, the leader takes the responsibility for results. Someday you'll be charged with building a marriage relationship and a family. It's the most important responsibility you will have on this earth. I know you will do well.

ON THE PATH TOWARD HONOR

1. What leadership qualities are you developing in your life now? How will these qualities carry over into your role as head of a family? What areas need

some work?

2. Have you made daily Bible reading and prayer a priority? What are your convictions concerning the importance of spending time with God? How do you plan to establish and maintain a Bible study time with your family?

3. Are you able to share your leadership with others when necessary? Do you seek and listen to wise advice when it is offered? How will your attitude toward leadership affect the 100/100 effort necessary for a strong marriage?

18
DESTINY
❦

Becoming a Man of Honor

For I know the plans I have for you, says the Lord.
They are plans for good and not for evil, to give you
a future and a hope. In those days when you pray, I
will listen. You will find me when you seek me, if
you look for me in earnest.

(Jeremiah 29:11-13)

A quotation I read recently on a man's T-shirt speaks to the world's values: "The man with the most toys wins."

As a man of destiny, your planning horizon should have a view of the Judgment Seat of Christ where our worldly works will be rolled before us and given a stare by the fiery eyes of a righteous God. The fire of testing will burn away all the works that don't count. What's left will be the works we did on earth that advanced the kingdom. The Bible says these works will remain as "gold, silver and precious stones." But the "wood, hay and stubble" will be burned away.

From God's perspective, the T-shirt would read:

"The man who does God's work wins." Even in a troubled world, your job as a Christian steward is to manage all the resources God gives you in a way that advances the cause of Christ.

Recent news provides us with more signs that man can't control his own destiny. Try as they might, the treasury secretaries of the most powerful nations cannot control the price of their currencies. The dollar's fall against the yen has the Japanese up in arms.

In Washington, politicians are using AIDS as a major issue in their TV appearances as they posture for the next election. Tens of millions of people will die of this disease in the next two decades, according to a recent study.

The budget deficit isn't coming down and neither is government spending. A greedy public demands more and more from government, borrowing more and more from future generations.

The schools are offering contraceptives as the solution to teen pregnancy, and they are trying to teach that man is a product of a chance mix of organic matter millions of years ago. Drug abuse in the armed services threatens our national security.

How can you get an optimistic view in a world so troubled?

There's only one answer: See it from God's perspective. His Word tells us that as we approach the end times, trouble will come. What we are seeing is evidence that God's timetable is in order.

One day the Lord will come to take Christians to be with Him. In His set time our works will be judged, we will reign with Him, and then begin eternity in heaven. The troubles of our times are for just a little while, until the remainder of God's plan for planet earth is played out.

The trouble you hear about on the evening news is just further indication that our time to complete the work God has left for us is coming to an end.

The world's troubles are all opportunities for us because prospering people with no problems have no time for God. Troubled times open up opportunities to talk about God's solutions.

So, there are at least two reasons to be positive. First, we know God's plan and how it is going to turn out. Second, the trouble in the world and in people's lives causes us to realize our need for God.

At the heart of the problems outlined on the evening news is the struggle between the forces of good and evil. That battle dates back to Lucifer's expulsion from heaven and Satan's tempting of Eve in the Garden of Eden.

The battle takes on many shapes and forms. At the international level, it's a war between those nations who believe God is supreme and those who believe man controls his own destiny. With the turmoil in politics, it is difficult sometimes to determine on which side of that battle line a country stands.

It's easy to place nations like China and Russia in the camp which denies the power of God. But what about America? She used to stand as one nation "under God." Now, with legalized abortion and laws which take prayer out of the classroom and creation out of the textbooks, we are in the midst of a drift toward the side which denies God.

The beginning of this drift to worship man as a

creature who controls his own destiny probably dates back to Darwin's theory of evolution. Perhaps it began with the Age of Enlightenment when the scientific method led man to believe that fact could be established only by empirical data.

The drift was slow. Wars of the nineteen-teens, thirties and forties, followed by Korea and Vietnam, led to the frequently quoted phrase, "There are no atheists in foxholes." But in the seventies the drift accelerated. Americans legalized abortion. Atheists pushed God out of the schools and Christmas decorations off the courthouse lawn.

Lewdness on TV in the eighties drifted to what would have been called pornographic in the fifties. And pornography, in the form of home videos and skin magazines, has become the hottest-selling item at the corner convenience store.

Homosexuals who were called perverts and queers in the fifties got their "gay rights" in the seventies and have become a political force in the eighties.

The rate at which society is sinking into sin and turning from God is increasing. To make a mark on this world, you must be willing to buck the trend.

Be All the Man God Wants You to Be

To be all the man God wants you to be, you only need to yield yourself to Him. Let God show you where you can play a role in the battle between God and Satan.

There's an inner battle going on in which Satan wants to puff you up and delude you into thinking that you are the champion of your own soul. As a Christian, though, you have the Holy Spirit bidding for control of your life. Hundreds of little choices you make every day will add up to become the major thrust of your life.

Generally, you will serve God or you will serve Satan. You can serve Satan in some ways which appear to be totally innocent. If Satan can use the things of the world to distract you from God's work, you are in his army.

The things in life which most people struggle for — money, power, recognition, influence, cars, houses, boats — aren't negative in themselves. But if these things become "gods" to you, they can ruin your chance to be a man of destiny.

On the other hand, if you use everything God gives you to advance the cause of His kingdom, He will give you more so you can invest more. If you have a servant's attitude, God will trust you to manage more and more of His resources.

To use your resources properly, keep the big battle in mind. If you are led to political activity use your influence to encourage candidates to take a stand on such issues as abortion, government control of individual's lives and overspending.

Use the influence God gives you to proclaim the name of Jesus Christ in the marketplace. Invite friends to gatherings of Christian businessmen. Be active in local evangelistic campaigns. Take a keen interest in foreign missions. Help as many of God's workers as you can.

But most of all, God wants you. He wants you to influence your family for Him. He wants you to be an effective member in the local church and in the body of Christ.

There are so many people with so many problems that can be solved only by developing a personal relationship with Jesus Christ. As I travel troubled America, I'm impressed with the number of people who, in the midst of economic turmoil, have turned to God. I hear some say, "I lost it all, but deepened my relationship with the Lord." Others have said, "I might never have met Christ had I not been in economic trouble."

Trouble has visited nearly every industry in America in the past decade — steel, real estate, construction, farming, energy, manufacturing and exporting of all types. The economy has reeled from high inflation to rapid deflation. This kind of uncertainty is pointing out to people that they can't put their trust in things. Only God is unchanging.

We could be seeing the beginnings of a great revival. Internationally, missionaries tell us the hunger for the gospel has never been greater. There appears to be a "window of opportunity" worldwide.

My advice to you is to be a man of destiny. Help change America's course of drifting deeper and deeper into sin and closer and closer toward depending on a powerful central government to solve all the problems of the individual. This drift away from God started with a few people changing direction.

Add the influence of your God-given resources to causes which uplift the name of Jesus Christ before men. That's what life is all about.

To be all the man God wants you to be, you must keep your eye on eternity. A man of destiny judges his life in the light of eternal values, not by counting the worldly toys he accumulates.

Son, your mom and I want God's best for you.

We want you to become the man God designed you to be — a man of honor.

ON THE PATH TOWARD HONOR

1. What (or who) in your life holds a danger of becoming your "god"? What are the signs that you've replaced God with something else in your life? What steps do you need to take to put God back in control?

2. What indications of a drift away from God do you see in our society today? What have been the forces behind this drift? In what ways have you been swept into this drift?

3. Can one person make a difference? How do you view your destiny in light of the individual influence you possess? How will you make a difference this week?

ON THE PATH TOWARD HONOR

Notes

Chapter 9

1. Larry O'Nan, *Giving Yourself Away* (San Bernardino, CA: Here's Life Publishers, 1984), adapted.

Chapter 16

1. Dennis and Barbara Rainey, *Building Your Mate's Self-Esteem* (San Bernardino, CA: Here's Life Publishers, 1986), pp. 27,28.
2. Don Meredith, *Becoming One* (Nashville, TN: Thomas Nelson, Inc., 1979), adapted.
3. Rainey, *Building*, p. 53. Used by permission.

Chapter 17

1. Elisabeth Elliot, *The Mark of a Man* (Old Tappan, NJ: Fleming H. Revell, Co., 1981), n.p.

List of Resource Books

The Holy Bible.

Blanchard, Charles A. *Getting Things From God.* Wheaton, IL: Victor Books, 1985.

Blue, Ron. *Master Your Money.* Nashville, TN: Thomas Nelson Publishing, 1986.

Bright, Bill. *How to Experience God's Love and Forgiveness.* San Bernardino, CA: Campus Crusade for Christ, 1971.

------. *The Holy Spirit.* San Bernardino, CA: Here's Life Publishers, 1980.

Burron, Arnold and Creins, Jerry. *Managing Stress.* Wheaton, IL: Tyndale House Publishers, 1986.

Christenson, Evelyn. *Gaining Through Losing.* Wheaton, IL: Victor Books, 1980.

Douglas, Mack R. *How to Make a Habit of Succeeding.* Grand Rapids, MI: Zondervan Books, 1966.

Elliot, Elisabeth. *The Mark of a Man.* Old Tappan, NJ: Fleming H. Revell, 1981.

Friesen, Garry and Maxon, J. Robin. *Principles for Decision Making.* Portland, OR: Multnomah Press, 1984.

Getz, Gene A. *Sharpening the Focus of the Church.* Chicago, IL: Moody Press, 1974.

Hart, Archibald D. *Adrenalin and Stress.* Waco, TX: Word Books, 1985.

Jensen, Ron. *How to Succeed the Biblical Way.* Wheaton, IL: Tyndale House Publishers, 1981.

Lutzer, Erwin W. *When a Good Man Falls.* Wheaton, IL: Victor Books, 1985.

MacArthur, John F. Jr. *Keys to Spiritual Growth.* Old Tappan, NJ: Fleming Revell, 1976.

Maxwell, John C. *Your Attitude: Key to Success.* San Bernardino, CA: Here's Life Publishers, 1984.

Meredith, Don. *Becoming One.* Nashville, TN: Thomas Nelson Publishers, 1976.

O'Nan, Larry. *Giving Yourself Away*. San Bernardino, CA: Here's Life Publishers, 1984.

Ogilvie, Lloyd John. *The Beauty of Sharing*. Eugene, OR: Harvest House Publishers, 1981.

Rainey, Dennis and Barbara. *Building Your Mate's Self-Esteem*. San Bernardino, CA: Here's Life Publishers, 1986.

Rice, John R. *Prayer: Asking and Receiving*. Murfreesboro, TN: Sword of the Lord Publishers, 1942.

Rush, Myron. *Management: A Biblical Approach*. Wheaton, IL: Victor Books, 1957.

Sanders, J. Oswald. *The Pursuit of the Holy*. Grand Rapids, MI: Zondervan Books, 1972.

-----. *Spiritual Leadership*. Chicago, IL: Moody Press, 1957.

Solomon, Charles R. *Handbook to Happiness*. Wheaton, IL: Tyndale House Publishers, 1971.

Stedman, Ray. *Authentic Christianity*. Waco, TX: Word Publishing, 1977.

Swindoll, Charles R. *Encourage Me*. Portland, OR: Multnomah Press, 1982.

-----. *For Those Who Hurt*. Portland, OR: Multnomah Press, 1977.

-----. *Recovery: When Healing Takes Time*. Waco, TX: Word Books, 1985.

-----. *Starting Over*. Portland, OR: Multnomah Press, 1977.

-----. *Stress*. Portland, OR: Multnomah Press, 1981.

-----. *Three Steps Forward Two Steps Back*. New York: Bantam Books, 1982.

Zigler, Zig. *Top Performance*. Old Tappan, NJ: Fleming H. Revell, 1986.

Worldwide Challenge *magazine helps you reach your world for Christ...*

* *through insights from Christian leaders and authors like Elisabeth Elliot, Bill Bright, Chuck Colson, Kay Arthur, Chuck Swindoll and others;*

* *through articles about people like you—home makers, businessmen, mothers, executives, professionals, singles—who are being used of God in extraordinary ways;*

* *through ideas about how to host a Jesus birthday party for children, how to take a stand for righteousness and how to tell your co-workers about Christ;*

* *through stories of Campus Crusade for Christ ministries around the world, imparting a vision to you for the world and giving you ideas on how to pray for those missionaries and new believers.*

■ *Special Introductory Offer!*

Order your subscription to Worldwide Challenge *magazine at the special introductory price of $7.95 per year. That's $2.00 off the normal $9.95 rate.*

Name_____

Address_____

City_____ State_____ Zip_____

I wish to pay by: ☐ *Check* ☐ *Mastercard* ☐ *Visa*

Card No._____ Expires_____

Authorized Signature _____

Mail to: Worldwide Challenge magazine, Subscriptions
Coordinator, P.O. Box 6710, San Bernardino, CA 92412

More Life-Changing Books

From  **Here's Life Publishers**

FATHER TO SON:
BECOMING A MAN OF HONOR
Merrill J. Oster

A fourth-generation farmboy turned communications company president shares timeless insights with his son on being a man of God in everything from handling finances to choosing a life partner. 0-89840-192-5/$6.95

MOTHER TO DAUGHTER:
BECOMING A WOMAN OF HONOR
Marilyn Willett Heavilin

The author of *Roses in December,* a former high school counselor, draws on experiences as a wife, mother and popular speaker as she explains how to be a woman of God in today's world.
0-89840-193-3/$6.95

"GOD IS NOT FAIR"
Joel A. Freeman

How to come to terms with life's "raw deals." Sensitive, straightforward help from a pastor and licensed counselor.
0-89840-189-5/$5.95

THE HIDDEN STRENGTH
Ingrid Trobisch

The wife of the popular late author Walter Trobisch shows how a deep commitment to the Lord can help you weather the storms of life. 0-89840-200-X/$6.95

SHOULD WE ALLOW MOTHER TO DIE?
Dorothea Marvin Nyberg

Biblical compassion and the terminally ill – how to face the dilemmas of caregiving and life support. Includes a helpful section on how to lead a terminal loved one to the Lord.
0-89840-203-4/$7.95

BUILDING A RELATIONSHIP THAT LASTS
Dick Purnell

A popular speaker at young adult seminars helps singles find the glue that cements relationships in order to avoid on-again, off-again relationship cycles. Part of the Dynamic Relationships Series. 0-89840-059-7/$6.95

WHAT CAN A MOTHER DO?
FINDING SIGNIFIGANCE AT HOME AND BEYOND
Judy Douglass

The author shares how she and dozens of other women have learned to achieve personal significance through a successful balance of mothering and ministry. For mothers of all ages.
0-89840-201-8/$6.95